Praise for *Profit or Growth?*

"A continuous renewal of the firm's businesses is essential for driving its profitable growth. This book gives credible insights and rich examples on how these renewal strategies can be shaped and executed successfully. I am recommending it to my key managers and business friends—essential reading!"

Peter Brabeck-Letmathe, Chairman & CEO, Nestlé

"To create economic value all enterprises have to achieve sustainable and profitable growth. Chakravarthy and Lorange explore this crucially important and equally exciting challenge. They capture well Novartis' strategy, which focuses on innovation and our core value of bringing novel medicines to patients. Our success is fundamentally built on our alignment and the passion and creativity of our scientists, which has enabled us to discover and develop groundbreaking therapies, such as our cancer medicine Glivec."

Dr. Daniel Vasella, Chairman and Chief Executive Officer, Novartis AG

"Sustaining both profit and growth requires the continuous reinvention of the enterprise. Bala and Peter have brilliantly captured the essence of this process, moving us beyond the myths to practicalities. As they point out, unleashing the firm's entrepreneurial energy requires coordinated effort by front-line, middle, and top management. Managers at all levels in the organization will gain learnings from their insights."

Brad Anderson, Vice Chairman and CEO, Best Buy

"The simultaneous pursuit of growth and profitability is one of the most exquisite—and difficult—leadership dilemmas. Bala Chakravarthy and Peter Lorange provide penetrating insights and persuasive real-life examples on how a company can address this dilemma through continuous renewal and internal entrepreneurship. Unusual for books on leadership, their discussion spans from theory through practical implementation."

Nick Shreiber, Former President & CEO, Tetra Pak Group

"Bala Chakravarthy and Peter Lorange bring new useful insight to the leadership strengths required in continuously renewing companies."

Matti Alahuhta, CEO, Kone

PROFIT OR GROWTH?

|||| Wharton School Publishing

In the face of accelerating turbulence and change, business leaders and policy makers need new ways of thinking to sustain performance and growth.

Wharton School Publishing offers a trusted source for stimulating ideas from thought leaders who provide new mental models to address changes in strategy, management, and finance. We seek out authors from diverse disciplines with a profound understanding of change and its implications. We offer books and tools that help executives respond to the challenge of change.

Every book and management tool we publish meets quality standards set by The Wharton School of the University of Pennsylvania. Each title is reviewed by the Wharton School Publishing Editorial Board before being given Wharton's seal of approval. This ensures that Wharton publications are timely, relevant, important, conceptually sound or empirically based, and implementable.

To fit our readers' learning preferences, Wharton publications are available in multiple formats, including books, audio, and electronic.

To find out more about our books and management tools, visit us at whartonsp.com and Wharton's executive education site, exceed.wharton.upenn.edu.

PROFIT OR GROWTH?

Why You Don't Have to Choose

Bala Chakravarthy

Peter Lorange

Vice President, Editor-in-Chief: Tim Moore
Associate Editor-in-Chief and Director of Marketing: Amy Neidlinger
Wharton Editor: Yoram (Jerry) Wind
Acquisitions Editor: Martha Cooley
Editorial Assistant: Pamela Boland
Digital Marketing: Julie Phifer
Publicist: Amy Fandrei
Marketing Coordinator: Megan Colvin
Cover Designer: Chuti Prasertsith
Managing Editor: Gina Kanouse
Copy Editor: Keith Cline
Proofreader: Karen A. Gill
Indexer: Lisa Stumpf
Compositor: Bronkella Publishing LLC
Manufacturing Buyer: Dan Uhrig

⅏ Wharton School Publishing

© 2008 by Pearson Education, Inc.
Publishing as Wharton School Publishing
Upper Saddle River, New Jersey 07458

Wharton School Publishing offers excellent discounts on this book when ordered in quantity for bulk purchases or special sales. For more information, please contact U.S. Corporate and Government Sales, 1-800-382-3419, corpsales@pearsontechgroup.com. For sales outside the U.S., please contact International Sales at international@pearsoned.com.

Printed in the United States of America

First Printing September 2007

ISBN-10: 0-13-233952-8
ISBN-13: 978-0-13-233952-0

Pearson Education LTD.
Pearson Education Australia PTY, Limited.
Pearson Education Singapore, Pte. Ltd.
Pearson Education North Asia, Ltd.
Pearson Education Canada, Ltd.
Pearson Educatión de Mexico, S.A. de C.V.
Pearson Education—Japan
Pearson Education Malaysia, Pte. Ltd.

Library of Congress Cataloging-in-Publication Data

Chakravarthy, Bala.

Profit or growth? : why you don't have to choose / Bala Chakravarthy, Peter Lorange.

  p. cm.

  ISBN 0-13-233952-8 (hardback : alk. paper) 1. Strategic planning. 2. Organizational effectiveness. 3. Industrial management. 4. Success in business. I. Lorange, Peter. II. Title.

  HD30.28.C438 2008

  658.4'012--dc22

2007014612

To my mother Sushila, for launching me on a growth journey, and to my wife, Kiran, for inspiring my continuous renewal.
—Bala

To Countess Ebba Wachtmeister, who passed away so prematurely.
—Peter

Contents

About This Book

In Chapter 1, "The Performance Dilemmas," we describe the performance dilemmas that confront firms and the underlying strategy and execution challenges that executives must successfully meet to address these dilemmas. The book is organized in two parts: Part I devoted to strategy, Part II to execution.

Part I: Strategy

In Chapters 2, 3, and 4, we develop the continuous renewal framework. In Chapter 2, "Renewal Strategies," we describe four renewal strategies. The first two are the traditional strategies of protecting and extending the current core business of the firm and transforming the firm in search of opportunities and capabilities that are distant from the core. We advocate the use of two bridging strategies (build and leverage) that help diversify the firm's core, but in more evolutionary ways.

Protect and extend, transform, build, and leverage are not competing strategies, but rather complementary elements in a shared strategic architecture. In Chapter 3, "Continuous Renewal," we explain how the latter two can be combined to ensure continuous renewal and sustain profitable growth.

In Chapter 4, "A Blended Approach," we emphasize the supporting roles that organic growth, acquisitions, and alliance play in executing the four renewal strategies. These are three means to implement a chosen strategy, not strategies in their own right.

Part II: Execution

In Chapters 5, 6, and 7, we focus on the execution of renewal strategies. The focus is on organic growth and on the multilevel effort required.

In Chapter 5, "The Entrepreneur-Manager," we profile the entrepreneur-manager—the prime mover of the renewal effort—and describe the personal traits, professional skills, and experiences of a successful entrepreneur-manager.

In Chapter 6, "Sponsoring Renewal," we describe the important role that senior executives play in defining the renewal agenda, finding the entrepreneur-manager to run it, locating a suitable organizational home for the project, creating a supportive context to aid its implementation, and coaching the entrepreneur-manager to success. Having effective sponsors is important for developing and retaining good entrepreneur-managers.

In Chapter 7, "Directing Renewal," we examine the role of top management in providing the overarching vision, values, and culture to promote continuous renewal, and in managing the inevitable dilemmas in executing it.

We conclude the book with Chapter 8, "The Multiactor Process," providing an overarching view on how to sustain profitable growth. The appendixes to this book provide useful summary tables.

What to Expect

We do not provide simple do's and don'ts in this book. Driving profitable growth is simply not that easy. However, what the book provides is a realistic perspective on the multiple roles that have to be played successfully and coordinated effectively for sustaining profitable growth.

Top management naturally carries a large burden here. The roles that senior executives—business, regional, and functional heads—play in making this vision a reality is just as critical. They are the ones who identify what the right blend should be between efforts that are centered on organic growth, alliances, or acquisitions. The firm's organizational context is also set by them. Finally, the firm's entrepreneur-managers are the prime drivers of its renewal efforts.

Even though we have highlighted different roles in different chapters, we hope that, irrespective of their own roles, managers will see each chapter as relevant. After all, they are all actors on the same stage, delivering one script. They have to know and appreciate the multiple and coordinated roles that must be performed to sustain profitable growth.

Acknowledgments

In preparing this book, we have sought to iterate our empirical research with observations in the field and then to test and refine the resulting ideas in the various programs that we have taught at IMD. We hope you, the reader, will see the book as both well reasoned and practical; and for that we have several individuals to thank.

First, we appreciate the support that Royal Dutch Shell, Nestlé, and Best Buy have provided us. Bala, as the Shell Professor at IMD, and Peter, as the Nestlé Professor at IMD, have benefited immensely from their work with these two companies. Some of that work is presented in this book, but there is a lot more that has shaped our thinking and validated or challenged our hunches. Bala has also been associated with Best Buy for more than a decade and has watched this company reach the very top of its industry. There are many individuals in these three companies who have given very generously of their time. Although we cannot list them all here, we thank them sincerely. We are also grateful to Jeroen van der Veer, chief executive of Royal Dutch Shell; Peter Brabeck-Letmathe, chairman of the board and CEO of Nestlé; Richard Schulze, founder and chairman of the board, Best Buy; and Bradbury (Brad) Anderson, vice chairman and CEO, Best Buy, for their personal support for our work.

We have benefited as well from the experiences and insights of leaders in a number of other corporations. We would like to acknowledge in particular the advice that we have received from Bill George, the former chairman and CEO of Medtronic; Fernand Kaufmann, former group vice president for new businesses at the Dow Chemical company; Gerard Kleisterlee, president and CEO of Royal Philips Electronics; Nick Shreiber, former CEO of TetraPak; and Daniel Vasella, chairman of the board and CEO of Novartis.

We also owe a deep debt of gratitude to four special executives: Matti Alahuhta, CEO of Kone; Gerhard Berssenbrügge, CEO of Nestlé Nespresso SA; Michael Garrett, former executive vice president, Asia Pacific, at Nestlé; and Ed Marra, former executive vice president, Group Strategic Business Units and Marketing, at Nestlé. They not only shared their wisdom with us but also took the trouble of reading earlier drafts of the book manuscript and providing detailed and very constructive feedback. This book is immensely richer as a result. We are deeply saddened that Ed Marra is not with us today to see the final product.

On a project with a broad scope like this, we have had to rely on the fine work of others in the field, both at IMD and elsewhere. We have cited some of the important inspirations in the References section of our book. Our special thanks go to Kash Rangan, Bala's brother and a professor at the Harvard Business School, who helped sharpen the conceptual underpinnings of our renewal framework.

Also, we acknowledge here those who have helped us more directly in our research at IMD, our research associates: Henri Bourgeois, Alastair Brown, Hee-Jae Cho, and Abraham Lu; John Evans and his superb team at our Information Center for their help with data gathering; Gordon Adler and his ever-helpful editorial team; and Persita Egeli-Farmanfarma, for her help with case research. In addition, Bala would like to thank his assistant Jessica Savoyen, and Peter his assistants Eva Ferrari and Annette Polzer, for their magnificent administrative support.

Doing the research and producing the manuscript is just part of the journey; getting it ready for publication is an important and big step. Here we have to first thank our former colleague at Wharton—its Lauder Professor Yoram (Jerry) Wind, who is also the co-editor of Wharton School Publishing. The thoughtful reviews that he and his advisory team at Wharton provided have strengthened the academic credentials of this book enormously.

The editorial and publishing team at Pearson has been a pleasure to work with. We thank Tim Moore, Gina Kanouse, Martha Cooley, Laura Blake, and the Pearson team for their excellent help. We must acknowledge in particular the help of two outstanding individuals: Liz Gooster, our publisher at Pearson; and Stuart Crainer, our style advisor. They have helped us improve the structure and readability of this book immensely.

We have reserved our final and important thanks for our partners, who made all the sacrifices while we toiled on our project. Bala's wife, Kiran, a senior executive in her own right, read countless drafts and offered invaluable advice on all aspects of the book. Peter's partner, Ebba, was of tremendous support to him and unfortunately passed away before this book could be completed.

Although so many have helped on the book, we alone are responsible for any blemishes that still remain.

IMD   *Bala Chakravarthy* and
Lausanne, Switzerland   *Peter Lorange*

About the Authors

Dr. Bala Chakravarthy is Professor of Strategy and International Management and holds the Shell Chair in Sustainable Business Growth at IMD. He received his undergraduate education in engineering at IIT, Madras and his MBA from IIM, Ahmedabad. He worked as an executive at Tata Motors in his native India before earning his doctorate at the Harvard Business School. He has taught at the Wharton School and INSEAD, where he was the director of its corporate renewal initiative from 1993 through 1994. Most recently, Bala held the Edson Spencer Chair in Technological Leadership at the Carlson School of Management, University of Minnesota. He has won numerous awards for excellence in teaching throughout his career. Bala is also an active top management consultant and executive education specialist. He has worked in this capacity with a number of leading multinationals around the world.

Bala's research and teaching interests cover three related areas: strategy processes for sustainable business growth, corporate renewal, and leadership dilemmas. Bala has published four books, several case studies, and numerous articles on these topics in top journals. Bala has served or continues to serve on the editorial boards of the *Strategic Management Journal, Management Science* journal, *Long Range Planning Journal*, and the *Strategy & Leadership* journal. He was a member of the Board of Directors of the International Strategic Management Society from 1999 through 2004. He is also an inaugural Fellow of that society.

Dr. Peter Lorange has been President of IMD since July 1, 1993. He is Professor of Strategy and holds the Nestlé Chair. He was formerly President of the Norwegian School of Management in Oslo. His areas of special interest are strategy, global strategic management, strategic planning, strategic alliances, and strategic control. In management education, Dr. Lorange was affiliated with the Wharton School, University of Pennsylvania for more than a decade in various assignments—including director for the Joseph H. Lauder Institute of Management and International Studies, and The William H. Wurster Center for International Management Studies, as well as The William H. Wurster Professor of Multinational Management. He has also taught at the Sloan School of Management (M.I.T.), IMEDE (now IMD), and the Stockholm School of Economics. Dr. Lorange has written or edited 16 books and some 110 articles. He has conducted extensive research on multinational management, strategic planning processes, strategic control, and strategic alliances. He has worked extensively within his areas of expertise with U.S., European, and Asian corporations—both in a consulting capacity and in executive education. He serves on the Board of Directors of several companies including Christiania Eiendomsselskap A/S, StreamServe Inc., Preferred Global Health, Zaruma Resources Inc., Copenhagen Business School, Seaspan Corporation, and Terra Global. He received his undergraduate education from the Norwegian School of Economics and Business, was awarded a Masters of Arts degree in operations management from Yale University, and his Doctor of Business Administration degree from Harvard University.

CHAPTER 1

The Performance Dilemmas

"To cope with dilemmas is the nature of managerial work."

—*Gerard Kleisterlee, President and CEO, Royal Philips Electronics*

The Elusive Targets

A public company anywhere in the world is driven by two goals. First, it wants to be profitable, to record a return on invested capital that exceeds the cost of capital. Second, it wants to grow revenue. In an ideal world, it would sustain both profitability and growth over long periods. Why? Simply put, driving profitable growth enhances value for the firm's shareholders.

Although the merits of sustaining profitability and growth are obvious, achieving them is elusive. Evidence repeatedly suggests that few firms have been able to show sustained growth or profitability—let alone both simultaneously.

Look at growth. A major consulting firm found that even in the best of times (the boom decade of the 1990s), nine out of ten companies failed to sustain growth.[1] They could not meet even their own growth targets! Only 13 percent were able to grow as fast as gross domestic product (GDP) growth and inflation combined. Another study found that a mere 10 percent of publicly traded firms in the United States had experienced eight or more years of double-digit growth over the same period.[2]

If sustaining growth is hard, sustaining profitability appears to be equally difficult. A mere 5 percent of the 6,772 public firms surveyed in one academic study showed year after year a return on assets (ROA) that was superior to the average for their industry, on a sustained basis over any ten-year period from 1978 through 1997.[3]

As is obvious from the studies cited, there is no shared understanding of the benchmarks for profitability and growth and the time horizon over which these have to be sustained.

Some have used double-digit growth and profitability over ten years as a measure of sustained growth or sustained profitability. The rationale being that 10 percent return on invested capital (ROIC) would be needed at a minimum to cover the cost of capital; and, when corrected for inflation and GDP growth, the firm would need at least 10 percent annual growth to show any real growth in its revenue. There is no particular rationale for a ten-year horizon. It just seems long enough.

However, only a handful of industry subsectors—such as medical equipment, pharmaceuticals, oil and gas, semiconductors, and software—have shown double-digit growth and profitability over the recent ten-year period. Many have not. Because firm growth and profitability depend in part on industry performance, insisting on sustained double-digit growth and profitability for a firm might be too demanding a threshold.

Another approach is to consider the growth and profitability of a firm relative to the average for its industry. This has the merit of setting a more reasonable threshold for measuring sustained profitable growth, although it is hard to designate just one single industry for a diversified firm. At any rate, this is the approach that we have taken for our study.

We looked at the performance over a 15-year period from 1990 through 2004 of nearly 6,000 large public companies from around the world (see Appendix A, "The Empirical Study"). We examined the record of these firms in sustaining not just growth or profitability, but both simultaneously.

The results of our study were striking. Only one firm in four around the world was able to show sustained profitable growth over any consecutive five-year period. Moreover, for those that actually managed to achieve profitable growth, sustaining the two was incredibly challenging. Instead of getting easier, sustaining profitable growth becomes progressively more difficult as the time horizon is stretched. When we extend the time horizon to 10 years, the percentage of firms that sustained profitable growth drops to under 5 percent, and at 15 years it drops further to under 1 percent.

The conclusions are stark. Sustaining profitable growth is incredibly hard. It has proved to be beyond some of the best managers in the world and beyond some of the world's greatest companies. Nor does it appear to matter which industry sector a firm belongs to, how big the firm is, or which part of the industrialized triad (North America, Western Europe, and Japan) that it is based in. (The appendixes contain summary tables that show this.) This book seeks to answer two questions: *Why* is profitable growth so elusive? And, *what* can—and must— executives do better to drive profitable growth?

Tension Between Profitability and Growth

Looking through our research, there was something else that was eye-catching. When we began, we believed that profitability and growth were mutually supportive, the two elements of the holy grail of business success. But, the research uncovered discomforting tension between profitability and growth. More than 40 percent of the firms that achieved sustained profitability or growth failed to achieve the other (see Table 1.1). Instead of being mutually supportive, for many organizations growth and profitability are rival challenges.

Table 1.1

Sustained Profitability or Growth without the Other

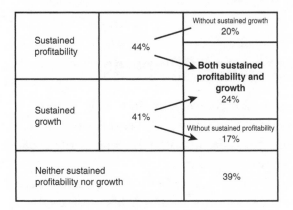

Indeed, sustaining growth can actually work against sustaining profitability—and vice versa. Consider the case of the global engineering giant ABB. After five years of losses, the company finally achieved its first full year of profitability in 2005, but at the expense of growth. Revenue had dropped over that period by an average of 0.6 percent each year.

Determined not to let the performance pendulum swing from a profit crisis to a growth crisis, Fred Kindle, the company's president and CEO, focused ABB around four performance measures: growth in orders and revenue; changes in operating margin—measured as earnings before interest and taxes (EBIT) as a percentage of revenue; capital efficiency—measured via both return on capital employed (ROCE) and return on equity (ROE); and the credibility and consistency of ABB's communications to its investor community. His aim is to emphasize profitability and growth simultaneously and to manage the expectations of the investor community around both. This is a daunting challenge, but it can be met.

Managing Performance Dilemmas

Webster's defines a *dilemma* as a choice between two unpleasant alternatives. Business dilemmas, uniquely, offer two equally valued alternatives. The unpleasantness lies in not giving one of the goals the attention that it deserves.

As the experience of ABB illustrates, enhancing value for the firm's shareholders is not as straightforward as it first appears. It requires the management of twin dilemmas: driving growth and profitability and seeking short- and long-term performance. Driving growth can hurt profitability (and vice versa), and sustaining both over the long term requires investments that can hurt short-term performance. No magic formula yields all four of these performance goals simultaneously. Tensions exist between them. These have to be balanced continuously.

A popular way to address the performance dilemmas is to tolerate periodic imbalances and try to correct them over time. For example, a company may focus on profitability for a period time and then focus on growth after it has accumulated a fair surplus. In our interviews, we often heard the expression "we first have to earn the right to grow" to euphemistically describe a profitability-first and then-growth approach to managing performance dilemmas.

In some contexts, this sequential approach might be unavoidable. For example, when a firm is fighting for its very survival, profitability is a must, whereas growth is merely nice to have. That might have been the case, for example, at ABB. When the company had to fight bankruptcy in the recent past, it naturally focused on profitability at the cost of growth. We also encountered a few firms, such as the cleaning company ISS International, where it was growth-first—to build the firm's market share, followed by a push for profitability.

However, our research shows that a singular pursuit of either profitability or growth makes it difficult to balance the two subsequently.

Pursuing growth requires exploring for new opportunities and competencies. It calls for entrepreneurship and risk taking. Profitability, on the other hand, is helped by exploiting the opportunities and competencies already available to the firm. Systems and processes fine-tuned to maximize profitability cannot nurture entrepreneurship.

Conversely, firms that focus on growth alone have trouble gearing their systems for operational excellence and improved profitability. Best Buy, the leading consumer electronics retailer in the United States, faced this challenge in the mid-1990s. It grew spectacularly with its innovative Concept II strategy, but its profitability was in trouble. It had to bring in outside help to fix its inventory-management and logistics systems. The company has since followed a more balanced approach to growth and profitability.

Moreover, the talent pool required to drive growth is often purged during the firm's single-minded focus on profitability. When the firm intends to grow later, it might lack the human engine necessary to drive this growth. This is the challenge some oil companies face today. When oil prices were depressed in the 1990s, oil companies laid off trained exploration and production engineers in their drive to maintain profitability. That very talent is in short supply today as these companies push for growth.

Under normal conditions, firms should strive simultaneously for both profitability and growth. The idea is never to lose the momentum for either growth or profitability, but always to balance the two. Our research shows that a simultaneous focus on growth and profitability builds a healthy momentum toward excelling on both over time.

Simultaneous Pursuit of Both Growth and Profitability

When we looked at the history of firms that had sustained both growth and profitability, on average, they achieved higher profitability and higher growth rates than either firms that sustained profitability (at the expense of growth) or sustained growth (at the expense of profitability). In other words, paying balanced attention to profitability and growth can actually enhance both.

Consider Medtronic. It is the global leader in medical technology—alleviating pain, restoring health, and extending life for millions of people around the world. In little more than 50 years, it transformed itself from a two-man garage operation in Minneapolis, Minnesota, to an $11.3 billion global enterprise in 2006, employing 36,000 people in 120 countries. The company's market capitalization stood at $62 billion in early 2007, representing a compound annual growth rate of 14 percent over the previous ten years. Its revenue in 2006 had grown at an average rate of 15.3 percent over each of the five preceding years. The firm has maintained an average profitability of 16.3 percent return on capital employed over the same period. Both numbers were among the best for its industry.

A number of factors have contributed to Medtronic's success, including its targeting of relatively unpenetrated markets, its distribution and market muscle, its constant drive toward new product innovations, and its select acquisitions of new growth platforms. A major trigger for these strategic initiatives, however, is the company's discipline in seeking profitable growth in each of its businesses.

Top management expects at least 15 percent growth from each of Medtronic's businesses—without compromising profitability. Stephen Mahle, president of the company's oldest and core business, Cardiac Rhythm Disease Management, explained:[4]

> *There is clear understanding everywhere in the company that it is in a growth business. This forces us to look at untapped opportunities.*

Indeed, the Cardiac Rhythm Disease Management business has matched the growth of the rest of Medtronic over the past five years.

This focus on profitable growth has percolated down the organization. A middle-level executive reflected on how this goal was monitored within the firm:

> *As a manager, you have to make your revenue budgets; that is definitely goal number one. And yes, you must also meet the bottom line. In a tough situation, they will let you have some breathing room, but you have to make the top line and show that you know how to achieve growth. The second thing you must do is to meet your earnings target. The real stars in our system meet their growth and profitability targets with great regularity.*

This simultaneous focus on profitability and growth is at the heart of how Medtronic adds value for its shareholders. It is a simple discipline and yet rarely followed. The obvious question is why.

Wisdom from the Field

To supplement our research into corporate data, we studied the efforts of several management teams around the world as they sought to drive profitable growth. Our work with European companies, including Nestlé, L.M. Ericsson, and Royal Dutch Shell—as well as the U.S. firms Best Buy, Dow Chemical, and Medtronic—has greatly influenced the ideas we present in this book. We have also benefited from the work of our IMD colleagues on companies such as Nokia, Canon, and Sharp.

Nokia, Best Buy, Medtronic, Nestlé, Canon, and Dow have sustained profitable growth in recent years (see Appendix E, "Major Firms in the Field Study"). We have gained insights from these companies. We have also learned from companies that have struggled. In addition, we have discussed our ideas with senior executives from numerous other global firms, in our capacity as researchers, teachers, and consultants.

We have learned a lot from two companies in particular: Nestlé and Best Buy.

Nestlé, headquartered in Vevey, Switzerland, is the world's largest food and beverage company. A 2004 Stern Stewart survey declared Nestlé to be the top-ranked European company, based on their twin criteria of top line growth between 1983 and 2003 and the market value that was added to the investment of the company's shareholders since its inception. Nestlé had a record year in 2005, with revenue of 91 billion Swiss francs, up from 84.7 billion Swiss francs the previous year. Its earnings before interest, taxes, and amortization of goodwill (EBITA) in 2005, at 11.72 billion Swiss francs, was also up by 8.9 percent over the previous year. Revenue was projected to grow at 9.1 percent for 2006, with profitability also slated to improve further.

Best Buy is the largest consumer electronics retailer in North America, with revenue of $30.85 billion in 2006. The company grew its revenue at an average rate of 17 percent a year from 2002 through 2006, and its profitability averaged 15 percent ROIC over the same period. In 2004, *Forbes* magazine declared Best Buy "America's Best Managed Company of the Year." Forbes applauded Best Buy's excellent performance in delivering a five-year annualized return of 26.5 percent to its shareholders.

We have worked closely with the CEOs of both companies and their senior executive colleagues. The accomplishments of the two leadership teams are truly impressive, but they're not flawless. They have had their own struggles. Sustaining profitable growth requires eternal vigilance and continuous hard work.

We want to abstract from the experiences of these and other companies that we have had the privilege to study and offer ideas for driving profitable growth.

Driving Profitable Growth

Addressing the Underlying Drivers

Consider the challenge that Gerard Kleisterlee, the president of Philips, faced in strengthening the company's profitability without compromising growth. When he became the president of Philips in April 2001, the company was still recovering from its brush with bankruptcy a decade earlier. Record losses in 2001, combined with a 15-year losing streak in the important United States market, called for a quick fix. Indeed, Kleisterlee took several immediate steps to boost the company's profitability, including selling nearly 30 noncore businesses with combined annual sales of about $1 billion, outsourcing the unprofitable production of cell phone handsets, and centralizing a number of service functions.

Even as Kleisterlee pushed for improved profitability, he had to lay the foundation for sustained growth. He defined four key themes in a technology future that Philips could win: display, storage, connectivity, and digital video processing. However, winning required abandoning the old silo mentality at Philips, and businesses had to cooperate across their divisional boundaries. He started sponsoring "strategic conversations" around each of the key technology themes, a one-day summit for key players regardless of their rank. These conversations led to clear goals, strategies, and road maps for key projects.

Five years into its transformation, Philips has achieved a remarkable turnaround. Its sales have started growing again, up to €30.4 billion in 2005 from a low of €27.9 billion in 2003 (when the noncore businesses were sold off). Its ROIC has grown healthfully from −11.7 percent in 2002 to 14.9 percent in 2005. It is beginning to see profitable growth.

For Kleisterlee, seeking profitability and growth meant investing in the core businesses of Philips and developing new businesses for the future (such as health care), driving efficiency and nurturing innovation, and insisting on strict deliverables from each organizational silo even when encouraging them to share freely with each other. Underlying the performance dilemma then was a cluster of other dilemmas that needed to be managed.

Unlike when making decisions, no alternative can be discarded when managing dilemmas. Instead, the two alternatives need to be balanced continuously. This is the balancing act that managers must learn to master if they are to sustain profitable growth. As Kleisterlee astutely puts it, managing dilemmas is the essence of managerial work. Sustaining profitable growth requires managing strategy, organizational, and people dilemmas.

Also, what we find from our field work is that just as in the making of an Oscar-winning motion picture, sustaining profitable growth requires a simultaneous attention to the script, actors, and set (see Figure 1.1). All are important, one no more important than the other. The script for sustaining profitable growth is the firm's strategy for continuous renewal. The actors are renewal-oriented managers at various levels who can shape and implement four complementary renewal strategies. The set is the firm's organizational context. It must support (and not hinder) the renewal efforts of its managers.

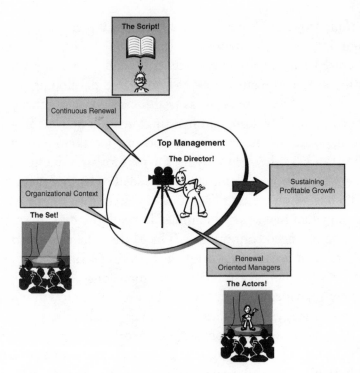

Figure 1.1
Driving profitable growth.

Continuous Renewal

A persistent dilemma for leaders is to offer a strategy architecture that allows the firm to exploit its existing strengths and opportunities while simultaneously pushing it to explore new opportunities and capabilities that will be needed for competing successfully in the future. It is a tension between ensuring profitable growth today and sustaining profitability and growth over the long run.

Winning today's competitive battles calls for investments that strengthen the firm's current capabilities. Invisible assets, such as customer relations or the network of resources and information that a firm commands, might not often make the list of a firm's core capabilities, but they should. They are important growth platforms.[5] Resources must also be allocated to initiatives that exploit these capabilities in geographies, products, value chains, channels, and customers that are adjacent to the firm's current opportunities.[6] But, will such a strategy also serve the firm well in the future?

Some experts have argued that competing for the future obliges the firm to risk its present.[7] Insisting on a link between the firm's present and its future may distract corporate leaders from delivering top performance and instead shift their focus to continuity and survival. Managing for mere survival does not generate strong long-term performance for the firm's shareholders. What the firm needs instead is a process that brings the discipline of external financial markets inside the firm and forces it to adapt speedily and radically to the changes in its environment. Leaders should be prepared to cannibalize the firm's products, make its core competencies obsolete, and retire physical capacities and human resources that are not needed. The firm should launch creative new products and services that can disrupt the market position of competitors, even if this means disruptions inside the firm, too.[8] Some have called this *creative destruction.*[9] Senior executives are intrigued by the radical views that the champions of disruptive growth have to offer. However, it is not clear what impact these have had on companies. The executives we have talked to plead that abandoning the present for an uncertain future is not that easy. After all, the firm's key customers, markets, and distinctive competencies are all embedded in its core businesses. To willingly give up these competitive advantages for unfamiliar terrain is risky. As an exasperated CEO put it, "My problem is not the present or the future; it is both.

How can I compete for the future without mortgaging my present?"

We believe that a firm can engage in a dramatic transformation, but through an evolutionary process, not a revolutionary one. The present does not have to be discarded; it can be morphed into the future. It is the preferred way to transform the firm without taking undue risks. We call this *continuous renewal.*

Firms such as Best Buy, Canon, Nestlé, and Medtronic that have sustained profitable growth are masters at continuous renewal. We tell their stories in this book. The first two have relied primarily on organic growth until recently, whereas the latter two have blended organic growth with acquisitions and alliances. Both approaches work. Debates over whether acquisition, alliance, or organic growth is the preferred way to drive profitable growth are meaningless. These are not strategies per se, but are means to implement four renewal strategies that we describe in this book: protect and extend, leverage, build, and transform.

Renewal-Oriented Managers

It is one thing to come up with renewal strategies, but it's quite another to detail and implement them. Managers who have become good at optimizing performance under today's business model might be reluctant to try anything new.

One way to address this problem is to insulate new renewal initiatives from a firm's core businesses and staff these with new hires who can connect more easily with new customers and build new capabilities. The firm will have, in effect, two classes of managers: one for generating near-term profitability and growth by optimizing the current business model, and the other for sustaining this profitable growth into the future by nurturing new opportunities and building new capabilities.

This segregation makes sense in extremely turbulent business contexts (such as in the technology sector). The firm might have to move away from markets that it dominates and competencies that it is distinctive in merely to survive. Intel's migration from memory chips to microprocessors is a good example here.

However, not all industries face discontinuous change; and even when they do, there are always pockets of continuity within them. What the firm needs in these situations are managers committed to changing the core, not by insulating themselves from the core, but by building onto and leveraging useful elements in the core. We call them *entrepreneur-managers.*

These managers differ from the firm's operating managers in an important way. They are outward focused, aware of the changes to their business environment, and willing to take risks in search of new opportunities and new capabilities.

But entrepreneur-managers are not mavericks. Unlike external entrepreneurs, they do not march to their own drum. Instead, they are true to the corporate vision and values, always keeping their creativity within the bounds of the corporate strategy. Moreover, they also look for ways to connect their initiatives either to existing markets that the firm participates in or the capabilities that it has presently. They take prudent risks.

We will elaborate on the important role that entrepreneur-managers play in implementing renewal. However, their success also depends crucially on the support of senior business executives. We also discus this important sponsorship role.

The Organizational Context

Having a good script and the right cast of actors is important, but without a proper setting, the actors can find it difficult to act out their script. Organizational context matters for successful execution. Implicit in the term *organizational context,* we include the firm's structure and supporting processes and systems.

We have already alluded to the fact that an organizational context conducive for driving profitability might not be helpful for achieving growth. The context needs to support both. For example, formal planning systems that are well suited to exploiting current opportunities and capabilities might not be conducive for exploring new opportunities or building new capabilities. Critics of formal planning systems, such as Professor Henry Mintzberg, have championed instead a more ad hoc and emergent process. What is required, however, is a balance between these two extremes of everything prescribed by senior management to everything improvised by their subordinates.

Moreover, this balance varies with the renewal strategy that is sought to be supported. One size does not fit all. We discus the important role that senior executives play in setting a context tailored to each renewal strategy.

Top Management: A Special Kind of Director

To ensure superior performance, top management has to oversee whether the firm has the right renewal strategies, an organizational context supportive of these strategies, and people resources to execute the strategies well. It is in that sense similar to the role of an Oscar-winning director—mobilizing the right script, set, and cast of actors.

However, imagine having to work within the constraints of the script, set, and pool of actors used to make the previous award-winning movie to now make the next award-winning movie. That is the challenge facing top management. It is constrained by the firm's past strategies and the inertia of its organizational context. It also cannot start afresh with a new human resource pool at each step in the firm's renewal journey. And yet, it has to sustain the firm's superior performance over the long term. There has to be a thread of continuity, but each sequel has to appeal anew to the audience. Balancing continuity and change is a key challenge for top management. We discus how this challenge can be met.

Renewal also requires a culture of sharing inside the firm. Promoting this culture is another important responsibility of top management.

Finally, to echo again the president and CEO of Royal Philips Electronics, Gerard Kleisterlee, it is the burden of top management to help the organization cope with the many dilemmas it will face in its renewal journey. Top management can use its enormous influence and power to provide the counterbalance when strategy, organization, or people priorities get out of whack.

PART I
Strategy

CHAPTER 2

Renewal Strategies

"You need to change at least as fast as consumer expectations. That's renovation. To maintain a leadership position, you also need to leapfrog, to move faster and go beyond what consumers will tell you. That's innovation."

—Peter Brabeck-Letmathe, Chairman and CEO, Nestlé

Organizations can perform only within the opportunities that have been assembled for them and the capabilities that they possess. Both opportunities and capabilities can erode over time. Mere exhortation or hard work will not result in sustained profitable growth. Rather, it is the responsibility of a firm's managers to ensure that it engages in a process of continuous renewal, seeking new opportunities and adding new and distinct capabilities. Commitment to profitable growth is also a commitment to continuous renewal.

Seeking sustained profitability triggers the reengineering of a firm's business processes and the trimming of its business portfolio. Moreover, sustained profitability is possible only if the firm has distinctive capabilities that remain superior to that of its competitors. Its managers must strengthen/complement the firm's failing competencies with new ones. A focus on sustained growth, on the other hand, helps the firm to look beyond current opportunities and to explore new markets. Continuous renewal is about renovation, innovation, and more.

We present in this chapter a framework to distinguish four renewal strategies. We describe each of these at some length. Each is risky in its own way. We discuss these risks.

Renovation and Innovation

Renovation is about protecting and extending a firm's existing market share. It is achieved through continuous improvements in operating performance. It also calls for new product introductions, new approaches to servicing the customer, and new ways of segmenting the existing market, but without diversifying the competence base of the firm or the markets in which it competes. Renovation provides profitability and growth in the short run.

Innovation, on the other hand, is about entering new markets and serving them using competencies that are also new to the firm. It stakes out a new business domain for the firm to grow profitably in the future.

Consider the coffee business at Nestlé. It is one of the company's core businesses. Nestlé is the world leader in instant coffee. First introduced in Switzerland, it became a big hit with American troops during World War II. The company's brand, Nescafé, is a household name in all corners of the world. The company's global market share in instant coffee is an impressive 60 percent. But the market for instant coffee is maturing. Nestlé believes in continuously renovating its core businesses. It also believes in innovating beyond the company's current core to ensure its future success.

For all its strengths in the instant coffee business, Nestlé is not a significant player in the much larger roast and ground (R&G) segment. R&G represents nearly 70 percent of the total market for coffee. In 1986, Nestlé launched a subsidiary to enter the R&G market with a high-end espresso coffee, Nespresso, sold in individually portioned aluminum capsules. Each hermetically sealed capsule contains 0.18 ounces (5 grams) of R&G coffee, specially designed to work in patented Nespresso machines to brew a perfect cup of espresso coffee at the push of a button. Nespresso is an innovation for Nestlé.

Rupert Gasser, a former Nestlé executive vice president, was fond of noting that a thin line separates renovation from innovation. Renovation and innovation span a shared spectrum. We would like to sharpen this spectrum by defining four distinct renewal strategies: protect and extend (essentially a renovation strategy), transform (an innovation strategy), and two important strategies in between: leverage and build. At the outset, we must point out that these are not four independent choices, but rather four linked strategies. A well-managed firm should pursue all four of the renewal strategies to sustain profitable growth, albeit with differing emphases as appropriate to its business context.

Traditional Renewal Strategies

The two traditional renewal strategies are shown in Figure 2.1. The matrix is defined by the two conventional dimensions: markets that a firm currently is in (or would like to participate in), and the distinctive competencies that it has (or seeks to access) to defend its presence in these chosen markets.[1]

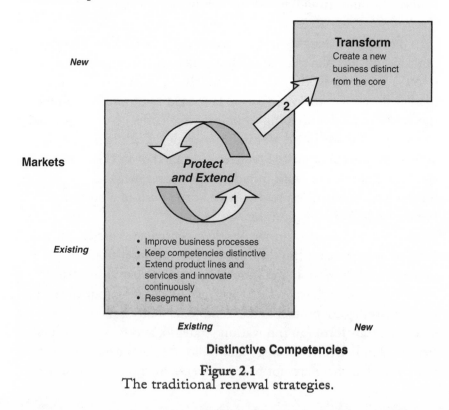

Figure 2.1
The traditional renewal strategies.

The term *markets* refers to the major market segments and geographies that a firm participates in. Nestlé, for example, defines its markets in terms of customer sectors such as coffee, water, ice cream, infant nutrition, performance nutrition, health-care nutrition, pet care, frozen foods, and others. Each customer sector has distinct market segments within it. For example, in the coffee customer sector, there is a segment for instant coffee and another for the more traditional R&G coffee. Each segment has a defined set of customers and competitors. Nestlé is a major player in the instant coffee segment. Nestlé also operates globally and can define its markets by the regions or countries in which it operates.

Whichever markets the firm competes in, new markets are always open to it. Some of these might have to be created de novo by the firm, but others might already exist and are merely new to the firm. For example, when Nestlé entered the pet-care market and the water market, these were new to Nestlé, but the markets already existed. On the other hand, when Nestlé entered the instant coffee market in 1938, it had to create it. In 1930, Nestlé's chairman was approached by the Brazilian Coffee Institute and asked to develop coffee that was soluble in hot water and still retained its flavor. The answer was Nescafé, and a brand new market segment, instant coffee, was established.

Distinctive competencies are the second dimension.[2] These may be in the form of a firm's tangible assets—such as raw material reserves, plant, equipment, distribution channels, and other logistical assets—and intangible assets such as brand name or customer relations. They could also be in the firm's know-how—its patents and its knowledge and skills embedded in its people and processes. In short, any element that adds value can be a potential source of distinction, whether it is related to procurement, research and development (R&D), operations, logistics, sales, or support activities such as information technology.[3] Because competencies eventually lose their distinction, new distinctive competencies are needed both to protect the core business of the firm and to provide it with a platform to enter new markets.

Distinguishing Renewal Strategies

Markets and distinctive competencies are complementary dimensions in defining a renewal strategy. Renewal is not only a matter of exploiting available markets and distinctive competencies, but also about exploring for new ones.

The lower-left cell in Figure 2.1 describes the present core of the firm, the markets that it participates in, and the distinctive competencies that it currently has. Protecting and extending the core is the obvious first renewal strategy. The other strategy is proactively migrating to new markets likely to be attractive in the future and acquiring new competencies to lead in these markets (migrating to the upper-right cell in Figure 2.1). We call this migration transforming the core. Both strategies (protect and extend, transform) have been written about extensively. We review them briefly here.

Protect and Extend the Core

At the first sign of competition, some managers may abandon their core markets and competencies in search of unrelated diversification.[4] Recall the experience of Bausch & Lomb, a U.S. pioneer of soft contact lenses. It had steadily built its market share to 40 percent and outperformed Wall Street through the mid-1980s.

But when confronted with new competition in the late 1980s, its leaders abandoned the company's core in preference for electric toothbrushes, skin ointments, and hearing aids. This unrelated jump into new markets requiring new competencies proved a disaster.[5] A new management team has since divested the company's noncore businesses, but meanwhile the company has lost its market leadership. Its stock has dropped precipitously, and the company is currently struggling.

Protect and extend is a base strategy that ensures that a firm's core businesses remain strong and avoid the kind of misfortune that Bausch & Lomb has experienced. It is in part a defensive strategy. Improving operational efficiency is a key element of this strategy. At Nestlé, for example, under the auspices of a companywide initiative called GLOBE (Global Business Excellence), the company has launched a number of efficiency initiatives. GLOBE is also aimed at sharing best practices quickly across the many countries in which Nestlé operates. Target 2004+ was one such program, and it resulted in savings of around $2.4 billion. Operational Excellence 2007 is another example aimed at saving $2.3 billion in supply-chain costs over the period 2005 through 2007. FitNes is yet another cost-saving initiative aimed at trimming administrative expenses by nearly a billion dollars from 2002 through 2007.

Continuous improvements in operational efficiency are a must for renewal. However, protect and extend is more than that. It is also a proactive strategy aimed at keeping the firm's competencies distinct from those of its competitors and at continuously improving the firm's market share both through product innovations and market repositioning.

Keeping Competencies Distinctive

A competence is distinctive in a firm only if it is hard for its competitors to easily procure, imitate, or substitute that competence. In time, a firm's competencies will be matched by its competitors, as was the case at Bausch & Lomb. Companies such as Nestlé recognize this danger. As one Nestlé senior executive observed, "It is good to sharpen your claws every day."

For example, in the Nescafé business mentioned previously, there is an ongoing effort to strengthen technical competencies. The extraction process, the freeze-drying process, the aroma process, the decaffeination process, the foaming process, and innovative packaging are technical challenges that scientists and engineers associated with Nestlé's coffee business try to master every day. Behind every cup of coffee, no matter where it is consumed, is an impressive array of technologies. Keeping it distinctive is an important preoccupation at Nestlé.

Technology may not be the key competence in other businesses. Depending on how the firm chooses to add value, other elements of the value chain may be the key to competitive success. It is a useful practice for corporate leaders to ask the following during each strategy review for a business:

> What competencies are required for competitive success?
> What is the business leader doing to keep these distinctly superior to that of the firm's competitors?

Obvious as these questions might appear, often they are not asked. Another set of questions worth asking has to do with exploiting all available opportunities in the market fully:

> Is the business cross-selling and bundling the products that it offers to increase its market presence?

> What is the track record of product innovations? Is the business able to hold on to loyal customers?
> Is there a way to further segment the market? Are there microsegments that can offer opportunities for profitable growth?

We discuss how each of these approaches can extend the scope of the firm's core businesses.

Cross-Selling and Bundling Existing Products Creatively

This strategy seeks to take advantage of a firm's strong reputation, whether it is in a market segment or geography, to sell other products. Established multinationals, such as Nestlé, see their broad market presence across the world as an important competence. This global reach allows them to harness the profit opportunity of a new product, whether it is developed centrally or anywhere else within the Nestlé network, quickly through rapid rollout worldwide.

A related approach is to bundle complementary products and sell them as a package to boost both revenue growth and profits. Hewlett-Packard (HP), for example, has been pushing its printers, print cartridges, and printing paper as a composite bundle. The idea is to impress on the customer that there is a special quality advantage in using an HP cartridge or HP paper in an HP printer. The percentage margins on printer supplies are far healthier than even for the higher-priced printers.

Continuous Product Innovation

Continuous innovation not only ensures that existing customers remain loyal to the firm, but it also allows the firm to get a larger share of their wallet. Companies such as 3M have a formal process to spark continuous product innovation. 3M used to insist that 25 percent of its revenue in any given year should come from products that did not exist in its portfolio five years prior. It has recently upped that requirement to 50 percent of its revenue in 2010 coming from products that did not exist four years prior. This is not a gimmick. Continuous product innovation is vital to the company's protect and extend strategy. George Buckley, the company's current chairman, president, and CEO, tells his organization: "Never, never, ever make me-too products." He wants the company's new products to be highly innovative, with the potential for further extensions over their life cycles.

In the Nescafé business, Nestlé has introduced new product lines such as cappuccino, latte, and 3-in-1 (coffee, dairy cream, and sugar in ready-to-mix portions) to spark new demand among existing consumers. Regions where Nescafé expects to grow, such as Russia, India, and Southeast Asia, are put on a different "cruising speed" and given special attention to encourage growth in these markets. The products sold are tailored to local tastes in application centers located close to these markets. In more mature markets, the company has tried to enter new segments such as the youth market with products such as café au lait and ice coffee, the health-conscious market with Ricoré and Bonjour; provided new packaging such as the single-serve sticks; and entered new channels such as online shopping. Nestlé's joint venture with Coca-Cola in the tea business area should also help provide wider market access for coffee as an impulse beverage sold largely via vending machines.

Resegmenting the Market

A great example of resegmenting is the coffee store chain Starbucks. It grew throughout the 1990s at an annual rate of

55 percent, when coffee consumption in the United States was nearly flat, growing at a modest 1.3 percent. Starbucks had the genius to identify, within this apparently mature market, a microsegment of coffee drinkers who were willing to pay a whopping premium for a well-brewed cup of coffee served outside of the home in a pleasant environment.

Unfortunately, these microsegments are typically discovered by new entrants to an industry and not by incumbents. It was Starbucks and not Nestlé that found this special group of coffee drinkers. Nestlé has concentrated instead on opening Nescafé corners in supermarkets, hospitals, gas stations, and offices.

Market Share, Growth and Profitability

The various approaches to protect and extend we have described are aimed at increasing a firm's market share. That is vital for growth, especially in maturing markets. As the pioneering work of the Profit Impact of Market Strategy program shows, an important link also exists between market share and profitability. A Bain and Company study of 185 companies in 33 industries shows that firms that had parity in share with their competitors achieved on average a 14.3 percent return on capital. In contrast, firms that were very strong market leaders—enjoying a market share much higher than that of their nearest competitor— achieved a return on capital that was 11.1 percent higher. Building share in current markets can help both growth and profitability.

Transform the Core

In sharp contrast to the protect and extend strategy, a transform strategy does not seek to strengthen the core, but to move away from it. This strategy can be pursued in two different ways:

primarily through mergers, acquisitions, and divestitures; or through internal efforts at new business development.

Buying a New Identity

If the goal is to abandon the current core and seek something entirely new, it is best to pursue transformation through mergers, acquisitions, and divestitures (as Westinghouse or Monsanto have done).

Westinghouse abandoned its legacy as a leading electro-technical and diverse manufacturing company to become a media industry player and even changed its name to CBS, a firm that it had acquired in 1995 as part of this transformation. In turn, CBS was acquired in 1999 by media industry giant Viacom. Westinghouse Electric Company today is the name of the erstwhile nuclear power arm of the old Westinghouse, a pale shadow of its parent and now owned by British Nuclear Fuels.

Like Westinghouse, Monsanto walked away from its heritage in the fast-commoditizing chemical industry to become a life sciences company in 1995. Its CEO, Robert Shapiro, spent more than $8 billion in acquisitions and joint ventures by 1999 in pursuit of his mission to make Monsanto a leader in finding solutions to the growing global needs for food and health care. By 1999, the company's revenue from chemicals had dropped to zero from a high of $3.7 billion in 1994. In the same period, revenue from the agriculture business had jumped from $2.2 billion to $4.1 billion and in pharmaceuticals from $1.6 billion to $2.9 billion. In December 1999, Monsanto merged with the drug company Pharmacia-Upjohn. Subsequently, its agricultural business was spun off to form a new Monsanto company.

Dramatic transformations such as those at Westinghouse and Monsanto are rare, often involving multi-billion-dollar acquisitions and divestitures. Although they do reset the growth trajectory of the firm, convincing shareholders that such a portfolio switch is best done by the firm's managers rather than the shareholders themselves can be hard.

Internal Development of a New Business
Firms can also pursue less-ambitious transformations internally. A good example of this approach is Nespresso. It represented a major departure from the core Nescafé business.

Nespresso was developed outside the Nescafé business at Nestlé in a separate venture. It was very different from Nescafé on a number of dimensions. First, it was an R&G coffee that had to be brewed as opposed to Nescafé, an instant coffee. The technologies required were different. Besides, Nespresso called for its own patented brewing machine. Nescafé, on the other hand, could be produced by stirring coffee from a jar in a cup of hot water.

Nespresso was also a new business model for Nestlé, which had never sold machines before. The product was targeted at a very different market segment—higher-end customers—using a new set of competencies and new channels—distribution of the machines through department stores and capsules directly through the Nespresso Club. Nescafé, on the other hand, was distributed through mass-market channels. Finally, the Nespresso brand was promoted separately and sought to have its own distinct identity.

Nespresso is today a global business within Nestlé independent from Nescafé. It has grown impressively, generating revenue of 818 million Swiss francs in 2005. Although internal ventures such as Nespresso cannot transform the identity of their parents like the external acquisitions did at Westinghouse and Monsanto, they are important to the eventual transformation of the firm.

Two Important Bridging Strategies

Between these two extremes of protecting and extending the core
and transforming it, we propose two other renewal strategies,
leverage and build, that bridge these two (see Figure 2.2).

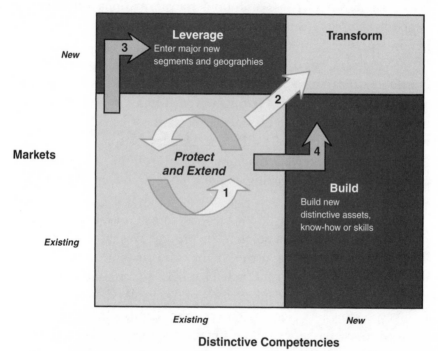

Figure 2.2
The two proposed renewal strategies.

The upper-left cell in Figure 2.2 describes new markets that the
firm can enter by leveraging the existing competencies that it
already has, but this is just the initial step. Complementary new
competencies will have to be added for the firm to compete

successfully in these new markets. Similarly, the lower-right cell describes the new distinctive competencies that the firm must build to protect its existing market franchise, but this too cannot be a dead-end initiative. The new competencies that are built must allow for future leverage into new markets. Both leverage and build should logically lead to the other (hence the bent arrows for leverage and build in Figure 2.2). If the two are linked systematically, they can help the firm migrate to new markets and new competence platforms progressively over time. Leverage and build are the two strategies that provide a fundamental building block for continuous renewal.

Leveraging the Core

"How do you put five Hondas in a two-car garage?" goes a popular question. The answer, of course, is that is possible only if Honda can sell a couple of cars, a motorcycle, a snow blower, and a lawn mower. Each of these products serves a different market segment but leverages the same Honda competence in making efficient and small internal combustion engines. That is a start, but for a leveraging strategy to succeed, the firm must add new competencies in product design and in distribution appropriate to this diverse range of markets. Leveraging is typically followed by build (the strategy that discussed next) and vice versa.

Entering New Geographies

Geographic diversification is an obvious leverage opportunity. The firm seeks to take its strengths in its home market to adjacent geographies, both nationally and internationally.

In a rapidly globalizing world, *adjacency* is defined not by geographic proximity but by markets in a similar state of development. Consider, for example, Dr. Reddy's, the Indian generic drugs manufacturer. It has deployed an international leverage strategy with great success. Countries in Eastern Europe, Southeast Asia, and Latin America were the first to be targeted with exports. However, the real targets were the big markets of Russia, China, Brazil, and Mexico. Dr. Reddy's started exporting to Russia in 1992 and subsequently set up a 76:24 joint venture there in 1995. The 51:49 Chinese joint venture became operational in 2001. The company has a subsidiary in Brazil and is planning to expand its operations in Latin America and South Africa.

Entering new markets is not enough. The distinctive competencies that help a firm's superior performance in its home market might not suffice to give it sustained competitive advantage in host countries. Dr. Reddy's has avoided that danger by consciously entering major new markets only through joint ventures. This gives the company a distinct local presence. It has also built a professional foundation of local employees in each major country. This is expected to contribute new skills and competencies to the firm and position it as a strong marketer in these countries, not only for its own products, but also those of other global pharmaceutical companies.

Entering New Market Segments
A healthy growth opportunity also lies in adjacent market segments that can be served at least initially with many of the distinctive competencies that the firm already has.

Consider Dell Computers. After its initial public offering in 1988, the company grew impressively by focusing on the business customer and selling direct. Then, in 1993, with a view to reach the home user, the company ventured into selling through discount retailers and wholesale clubs. Retail sales never grew beyond 10 percent and became a major loss for the company. Dell quickly withdrew from this segment; however, this was a temporary retreat. As part of its direct-selling strategy, the company embraced the Internet early. Even though this channel was also primarily directed at the business customer, Dell subsequently leveraged it to reenter the home-user segment. By 2006, the company's revenue had grown to $56 billion. In the United States, its largest market, Dell held an impressive 30 percent market share in this new segment. The company has now started selling high-definition TVs and other consumer electronics products to further strengthen its presence in the home segment.

The case of the U.S. multinational 3M is equally informative. It serves ten distinct markets, repeatedly leveraging its capabilities in nine technologies (see Figure 2.3).

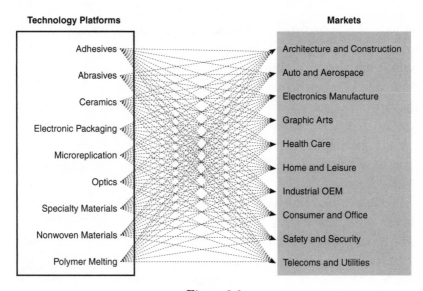

Figure 2.3
3M: Leveraging technologies into multiple markets.
Source: 3M

Consider adhesives technology, one of 3M's early competencies. The company has used this market-leading technology, together with others in its portfolio, to diversify into the consumer products and health-care markets. Or consider ceramics. These are nonmetallic materials that are extremely strong and temperature resistant. 3M first used them to create heat-resistant materials for the manufacturing sector and later leveraged that technology to market dental fillers and restoratives for the health-care market, durable reflective materials for the safety and security market, and colorful, long-lasting roofing material for the construction sector. By combining and leveraging the strengths of its existing competencies, 3M is able to experiment with entry into new customer sectors without major investment or risk.

Building the Core

All competencies of a firm are not distinctive. As noted previously, only those that are hard for competitors to procure, imitate, or substitute qualify as distinctive competencies. Again, this distinction cannot last forever. Competitors will either try to copy the firm's distinctive competence or even substitute it with something new of their own. Business history is full of examples of such substitution. In the 1970s, Digital Equipment took on the might of IBM by substituting minicomputers for mainframe computers; and they, in turn, were bested by Apple, IBM, and others with the help of microcomputers.

Unless the firm builds complementary distinctive competencies to defend its new leverage initiatives, it will have merely introduced a new opportunity for the second mover to make money. Research suggests that this is a common failure. Build is a strategy through which the firm adds new competencies both for defending its existing market franchise and growing into new markets. Unlike the protect and extend strategy, the intent here is not to strengthen a competence that already exists but rather to build a new distinctive competence.

Investments in build are hard for any single business unit to justify, given the long time delay between these investments and financial results. Sharing the investment with other potential business users makes it possible to build. They all share the risk. Corporate funding and oversight might also be needed to supplement these build projects.

Another advantage of sharing in a build strategy is that there are multiple users of the competence in waiting, as soon as it is built. Leverage follows naturally from build.

Consider how 3M pursues build strategies. Figure 2.4 shows how the microreplication technology has been progressively built (and leveraged) within 3M. One simple product, and a limited technology base in 1964, has evolved into a large array of technology capabilities serving eight applications areas.

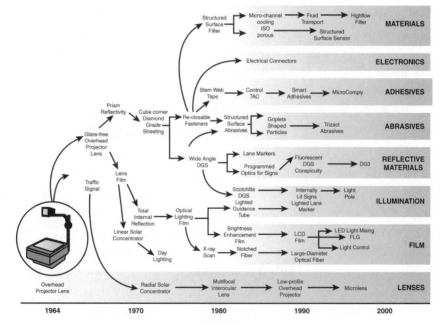

Figure 2.4
Evolution of the microreplication technology platform and markets for it within 3M.
Source: 3M

Proactively Building New Capabilities

Toyota's development of a hybrid car is a good example here. The technology for the hybrid car was developed for a niche segment of price-conscious consumers who were also actively concerned about environmental pollution from fossil fuels. The car was first taken to Toyota's main markets in the United States and Europe. In each of these markets, the technology was modified to fit local requirements. Toyota has since introduced a hybrid car in its higher-end Lexus range and in its sports utility vehicles (SUVs).

Another example is Nestlé's new low-fat ice cream. The company has invested in developing a new technology based on homogenizing low-fat milk and then extruding it into ice cream. This new technology was first tested at a Nestlé subsidiary (Dreyer, in the United States). Although the initial market for this low-fat product might be the United States, building of this competence has been motivated by expected market opportunities throughout the world.

Building Capabilities in Reaction to a Market Crisis

Consider, for example, Nestlé's battle in the yogurt market in Europe during the 1990s. It was facing very stiff competition from Danone, the French food retailer. Danone was a focused player, and in the categories in which it competed, it was a formidable competitor. In the early 1990s, Nestlé's central research laboratories in Lausanne, Switzerland, were working on the health benefits of a group of cultures called *lactobacillus acidophilus*. One of these cultures, referred to initially as LA1, seemed to have probiotic properties that were shown to help digestion, fight stomach ailments, and strengthen the body's immune system.

Yakult of Japan had already introduced a probiotic yogurt by then but chose not to take this innovative product idea global. The company was largely focused on its home market. Nestlé might have been inspired by the Yakult product success and set about developing its own version of a probiotic yogurt. Danone, too, was pursuing a similar product idea.

By September 1994, LC1 (the name changed due to registration issues) was introduced by Nestlé as a functional food—with the claim that it could strengthen the body's natural immune system.[6] The initial launch was not very successful. Nestlé's attempts to position LC1 as a health-care product that could strengthen the body's immune system rather than as a new food item may have cost the company valuable time. Nestlé executives acknowledged that although the science behind LC1 might have been close to perfect, the company's marketing fell short. LC1 was not a big success in the yogurt market, but it nevertheless contributed to building a new competence platform for the company.

Nestlé has since set up an independent nutrition division, focused on infant, health-care, and performance nutrition. As Peter Brabeck-Letmathe, Nestlé's chairman and CEO, notes, "It was clear that with tomato paste, oil, and dry pasta, I wasn't going to be able to create value in the long term. I had to identify platforms on which new growth can be built." Nutrition is a platform that he has decided to bet on. With industry sales stagnating, Nestlé is committed to building new competencies for competing successfully in the growing "phood" opportunity, a space where pharmaceuticals and food intersect.

Risks in Renewal

Renewal is not without risks. Clearly, transformation is the most risky; protect and extend is the least. Leverage and build are both moderately risky. However, failure to renew is also risky. Moreover, emphasizing protect and extend alone is also not the answer. We believe that complementing a protect and extend strategy with well-thought-out leverage and build strategies is the best approach to ensure continuous renewal without taking undue risk. Let's review the risks associated with each renewal strategy.

Risks with a Protect and Extend Strategy

There are four major risks with such a renewal strategy: imitation, obsolescence, complacence, and market saturation:

> **Imitation.** Competencies lose their distinction over time through imitation by competitors. Technologies can be reverse engineered and commercial ideas copied. Defending existing markets and competencies is not enough; these have to be continuously extended to keep the imitators at bay. We described the many efforts at Nestlé's Nescafé division to introduce continuously new technical inventions and commercial innovations to its product line. Failing to do so is risky—as Bausch & Lomb learned.

> **Obsolescence.** This risk is similar to that posed by imitation, except the focus of competitors is not on imitating a firm's competencies but rather on substituting them. A firm's competencies run the risk of becoming obsolete. Business history is full of examples of such substitution. We noted earlier how mini- and microcomputers substituted mainframe computing and ended IBM's monopoly in the computer industry. Or, consider the case of the virtual bookseller Amazon. It has successfully used the Internet to substitute the extensive brick-and-mortar distribution capabilities of Barnes and Noble. Paradoxically, the risk of substitution is the highest when a firm enjoys a dominant

market share, as the preceding examples illustrate. Challengers cannot possibly replicate the market leader's competencies; the only option they have is to make these redundant.

In dealing with the risks of imitation and substitution, it is useful to recall the famous saying of Andy Grove. The legendary CEO of Intel used to say it is only the paranoid who survive. Companies such as Intel obsolete their competencies before someone else copies or substitutes them.

> **Complacence.** This risk has more to do with ignoring market entrants who, if left unchallenged, can be formidable competitors down the road. Incumbents such as General Motors, Xerox, and Caterpillar were perhaps guilty of this risk, being dismissive of new entrants to their industry. Their challengers first went after segments that were not of much interest to the incumbents, thus keeping under their radar screen. But, in each of these competitive battles, the incumbent paid a huge price down the road.

It may be useful as part of a company's strategic planning process to designate a few devil's advocates to play the role of these upstart entrants and simulate where the firm's defenses can potentially be breached.

> **Market saturation.** A successful protect and extend strategy will eventually saturate a market, as in the case of Nescafé. Although continuous innovation and microsegmentation can pump new life into maturing markets, managers have to look at hard data and accept the eventual commoditization of most markets.

This risk cannot be managed per se, but by having other renewal strategies in the firm's portfolio, it can be diversified away.

Risks with a Leverage Strategy

Risks with a leverage strategy come from not understanding the needs of the customers in the new markets that the firm enters. This is often an underappreciated risk, especially when a firm is not just entering a well-established market that is merely new to it but rather seeking to create a brand new market opportunity. This was the case with Nestlé's LC1.

Nestlé's archrival in the yogurt business, Danone, chose to introduce its own version of probiotic bacteria in a yogurt drink called Actimel. It did not have a diverse product portfolio like Nestlé to get distracted with. It focused on one drink category and outspent Nestlé by an estimated three to one on marketing expenses. Danone's Actimel was a spectacular success when compared to LC1. By first positioning the product as a health supplement, Nestlé lost valuable time. Then in a rush to recover lost ground, it introduced LC1 in a variety of products, including pet food. By doing so, Nestlé reduced LC1 to a commodity ingredient.

Market development is risky. Consumers might not see the obvious benefits in a product that a laboratory scientist can, or consumers in one country might not quite care for the product features that were a big hit in another. As Nestlé recognized, it had mastered the science of probiotic bacteria but could not convey a meaningful value proposition around it for consumers.

The company has learned from that experience. For example, when Nestlé sought to enter the low-fat ice cream market, it knew it had mastered the technology of homogenizing low-fat milk and extruding it into ice cream. But leveraging requires connecting with customers and presenting benefits in a way that they can appreciate. The company has relied on Dreyer—a subsidiary that it had acquired in the United States—to help market an indulgent food like ice cream to a health conscious consumer.

First and foremost, managing the risks in a leverage strategy requires an understanding of customer needs in the new market. If a partner is not readily available to provide this insight (as Dreyer did in the low-fat ice cream example or the joint venture partners of Dr. Reddy's did in helping the firm enter the Russian and Chinese markets), the company will have to invest in market trials to bring down the commercial risks in a leverage strategy.

Risks with a Build Strategy

The risks with a build strategy come from difficulties in the competence development process. The new competence platform may be harder to build than first thought or more expensive than budgeted. Worse still, the anticipated uses for the new competence might not materialize.

Consider 3M's Optical Systems (OS) business unit. Founded in 1979, its mission was to find products for the company's light-control film that had been developed years earlier during its work with microlouvered technology.[7] Over the years, several other optical technologies became part of the unit, but OS continued to lose money for the next decade because applications for the various technologies were hard to find.

In 1990, after six months of research on a variety of potential areas where the film could be used, three were identified as offering the most promise: ATMs, museums, and sensitive computing. In all three scenarios, it was desirable that light be seen only from straight ahead. For example, someone using an ATM didn't want a passerby to see sensitive information. The OS unit began to push the privacy screen with mixed results. It estimated the total market at $200 million but only managed to bring in $10,000 a month. The business unit was shut down.

The OS business unit provides some important lessons for managing risk in a build strategy. The first is that it is always desirable to have a recipient market in mind before building a competence. It not only minimizes the investment risk, but it also provides a focus for developing the competence. Second, it would be even more desirable to develop the competence to first serve the needs of an existing market that the firm understands. Recall Dell's efforts at building an Internet distribution channel to first serve its business customers before leveraging that competence to go after home users. Finally, although managers must have the discipline to kill build projects that fail to connect with a market opportunity, existing or new, the competence that results should be preserved at a maintenance level for future use. 3M has recently reentered the privacy computing market, building on its earlier competence in optical screens.

Risks with a Transform Strategy

Companies face five major risks with such a renewal strategy: market development, competence development, financial, reputation, and disconnectedness. The market development and competence development risks are similar to those in a leverage or build strategy, except in a transformation strategy both market and competence development are attempted simultaneously, as in the case of Nespresso. The risks multiply exponentially.

Financial risk pertains primarily to transformations through acquisitions and divestitures but could also apply to internal development projects aimed at transformation. On average, acquisitions are expensive, and integrating the target is difficult. Whether it is Westinghouse or Monsanto or other such mega-attempts to transform the firm, the financial risks are huge. The track record of corporate leaders in pulling off these transformations is poor. Our advice is to avoid such attempts. If, for whatever reason, a firm cannot be renewed continuously, instead of attempting a heroic transformation through financial deal making, management is better off returning equity to the firm's shareholders.

A related risk, whether transformation is pursued through acquisitions or internal development, is the reputation of the firm. High-profile transformation projects attract a lot of media attention and, when they fail, the fallout for the firm can be catastrophic. Consider, for example, the reputation hit that Vivendi Universal took when Jean-Marie Messier's attempts to transform the company into a media giant from a "boring" water utility began to unravel. Even in the case of transformation projects that are internally developed, failure of the project has reputation risks for the firm. This is perhaps one reason why managers persist with transformational projects that are failing. Terminating them would also be to concede defeat and dent the firm's reputation.

A fifth risk that managers must contend with is the tendency of the new venture to become disconnected from the core. This isolates the venture from the firm's competencies and market access. Doing everything *de novo* magnifies the project's risk. Although the transformation venture needs to be given its own space and management attention, it also has to be connected to the core. That is one way to manage this risk.

Nespresso, for example, has relied on the technology and manufacturing competencies of the mother company. Whether it is in machine or capsule development to come up with that perfect cup of espresso coffee, Nestlé scientists and engineers are closely involved with the Nespresso project. Whereas the coffee machines are manufactured by licensed outside vendors, the coffee capsules themselves are produced in Nestlé's factories. Nespresso also gets Nestlé's help with shared services such as logistics, finance, and information technology. Apart from its first CEO, who came from outside Nestle, Nespresso (now called Nestlé Coffee Specialties [NCS]) has also looked to the Nescafé business for its two subsequent CEOs. Nespresso depends on Nescafé to support many elements of its value chain.

In turn, Nespresso can take Nestlé into a market space that it has not operated in before—the high-end consumer segment. It can also offer a brand new direct channel, the Nespresso Club. Its innovative commercial ideas may help the rest of Nestlé, too. Nestlé has built on the Nespresso idea to venture more broadly into "systems that deliver a choice of specialty coffee at the touch of your fingertips." It sold 6.1 million coffee-on-demand machines in 2005. These included the latest Nescafé Dolce Gusto machines—a new growth opportunity for the core Nescafé business.

A transformation strategy does bring new markets and competencies, but these might prove hard to integrate with the core businesses of the firm. Without these reverse synergies, the firm risks losing some of the financial value from its innovation. Instead of transforming first and then backfilling, a more logical approach is to start with the core and leverage and build from it.

Managing Risks in Renewal

Innovation is not about how distant a new business is in terms of its market space and distinctive competencies from a firm's core business; it is about how devastating the idea is to competition. In fact, the ideal approach to renewal is to make evolutionary moves inside the firm that have revolutionary impact on markets.

Instead of engaging in revolutionary transformation, with its attendant risks, a more prudent approach is to pursue a step-wise transformation through a judicious blend of leverage and build strategies. We are reminded here of a guiding principle that has governed the renewal of the Japanese company Canon. It has taken technology risks and market risks, but always one at a time and never both simultaneously. We will look at such a process in the next chapter.

Summary

Commitment to profitable growth requires a commitment to continuous renewal.

Renewal strategies can be defined by two traditional dimensions: markets that a firm currently participates in or wants to, and the distinctive competencies that it has or seeks to access to defend its presence in these chosen markets.

The two traditional renewal strategies are protect and extend and transform. Protect and extend is a strategy for profitable growth in the firm's existing market franchise through continuous improvements in operating performance, new product introductions, new approaches to servicing the customer, and new ways of segmenting the existing market, but without diversifying the competence base of the firm or the markets in which it competes. Transform, on the other hand, is about entering new markets and serving them using competencies that are also new to the firm.

We propose two additional renewal strategies that span the spectrum between protect and extend and transform. We call these leverage and build. Leverage is a strategy for entering new markets using the competencies that a firm already has. However, this is just the initial step. Complementary new competencies will have to be added eventually for the firm to compete successfully in these new markets. Build is a strategy of adding new distinctive competencies to protect the firm's existing market franchise. This, too, cannot be a dead-end initiative. The new competencies that are built must allow for future leverage into new markets. Thus, leverage and build should logically lead to the other.

Clearly, transformation is the most risky strategy. Instead of engaging in revolutionary transformation, with its attendant risks, a more prudent approach is to pursue a step-wise transformation through a judicious blend of leverage and build strategies. This will ensure continuous renewal of the firm and help to sustain both its profitability and growth.

CHAPTER 3
Continuous Renewal

"Those who build fortresses will lose—
and those who move on will survive."

—Hwang Chang-Gyu, president and CEO,
Samsung Electronics

Samsung Electronics is the world's leading maker of color televisions. It has overtaken Sony in sales revenue and has a market capitalization twice that of its role model. The company is building distinctive competencies in four core technologies: semiconductors, large-area liquid crystal displays, display drivers and chip sets, and mobile telephony. Samsung seeks to leverage these technologies to enter new market segments. It soon intends to be a strong number two to Nokia in the cell phone market, displacing Motorola; and it has ambitious plans to challenge Apple in the digital-music arena and HP in the imaging market.[1] Although there is so much to celebrate, its president and CEO gently encourages the company not to party but to move on.

Earlier, we laid out four renewal strategies: (1) protect and extend, (2) build, (3) leverage, and (4) transform. What Hwang Chang-Gyu, president and CEO of Samsung Electronics, seems to be arguing against is the bias that we see in the resource-allocation processes of many firms toward a protect and extend strategy. Samsung has chosen to be on the move permanently. It seeks to build new competencies and leverage them into new markets and do so continuously.

Strategies that seek to protect and extend the core can typically be justified under the current financial metrics in use. However, transformational projects are more risky. This raises the cost of capital assigned to them. Payoffs from these projects can come well into the future. The discount on these returns can also be very steep. Put these three factors together, and it is very hard to find a transformational project that will meet the hurdles of a conventional capital budgeting system. Take the case of Nespresso. It took the project 12 years to break even. Nespresso could not have been a positive net present value project under any set of reasonable assumptions.

However, Nespresso survived because it had the backing of Nestlé's top management. Indeed, top management intuition and support are essential if transformational growth initiatives have to be undertaken. Transformational projects are to be judged not as investments in the traditional sense, but more as financial options. If they work, they will provide the company a robust platform for growth, as Nespresso has done for Nestlé.

However, there is another, less-risky way to transform the company, an incremental approach such as the one that Samsung seems to have chosen. We call that *continuous renewal.*

Continuous Renewal

Continuous renewal calls for planned allocation of resources to a sequence of leverage/build initiatives (see Figure 3.1):

> Projects that pursue a new market opportunity aggressively but do so by first leveraging available competencies within the firm, and

> Projects that build new platforms of competencies to fuel future growth but do so first by strengthening the firm's competitive advantage in existing markets

The firm is transformed over time but through a sustained sequence of leverage (leading to build) and build (leading to leverage) strategies. Top management must have the stamina and dedication to persist with this effort through changes in its own ranks.

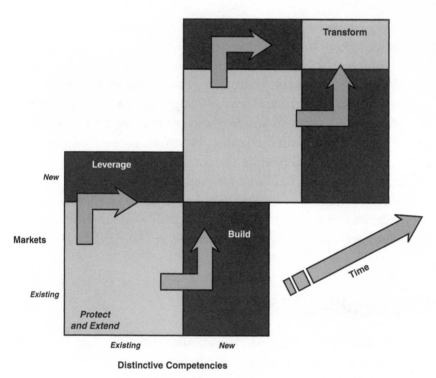

Figure 3.1
Strategy initiatives for continuous renewal.

An Exemplar: Best Buy

One company that has an exemplary record of continuous renewal is Best Buy, the U.S. consumer electronics-retailing giant.[2] In 2006, its 832 North American stores gave Best Buy the number one spot in its industry, with a 16 percent share of the $130 billion market for retail electronics and packaged media. The company has grown its revenue at a 15 percent compound annual growth rate since 1996. It has also achieved this growth with robust profitability. The company's total return to its shareholders (TSR) has grown steadily, outpacing the TSR growth for the Standard and Poor's retailing group as a whole. Even more impressive is the fact that Best Buy has achieved this leadership position in just four decades!

In 1966, at the age of 25, Richard (Dick) Schulze opened a small audio components store in St. Paul, Minnesota, called Sound of Music. Specializing in high-end audio equipment targeted at young males, the company grew steadily to 11 stores in Minneapolis/St. Paul by the early 1980s. Then, in 1981, a tornado tore the roof off Sound of Music's largest and most profitable store. Because the company did not have business-interruption insurance, family members and employees retrieved stereos and TVs from surrounding parking lots and fields and ran a Sound of Music "Tornado Sale."

The event was a spectacular success. Schulze saw in it the outlines of a new strategy. He would later refer to this as Concept I—focusing more on inventory turns than unit margins and making discount shopping a fun experience. Renamed Best Buy in 1983, the company has since pursued five more distinct strategy initiatives (see Figure 3.2), each called a *concept* in the company's jargon.

Each concept has helped the company expand its market scope or grow its distinctive competencies. In addition, the momentum for each concept has come from the previous one, with a steadily accelerating pace. Concepts I and II lasted six years, Concept III lasted three, Concepts IV and V just two. In 2004, Best Buy launched a sixth initiative, intentionally called Concept VII to signal that it was a quantum leap from the previous one. Best Buy today bears little resemblance to the Sound of Music stores of its early years, but its metamorphosis has not required a revolution. Instead, each concept has been an important link in the company's continuous renewal process.

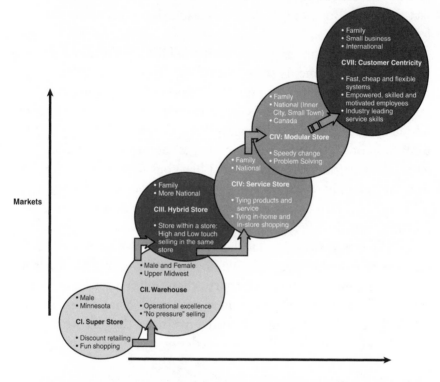

Figure 3.2
Four decades of evolutionary transformation at Best Buy.

Finding a Niche: Concept I (1983–1988)
This was a leverage strategy, seeking to launch a chain of superstores offering discount consumer electronics and relying on competencies that Best Buy had built in its Sound of Music

stores. Concept I sought to expand the company's geographic reach to cover the entire state of Minnesota. It was predominantly directed at the adult male shopper. In implementing Concept I, Best Buy learned how to service a chain of stores spread across hundreds of miles and acquired new competencies in managing quick inventory turns. Best Buy grew to 100 stores by 1988 using this strategy. That year, a regional rival, Highland Superstores, initiated a price war. Even though Best Buy had joined a buyers' cooperative to improve its own power over vendors, it could not match the aggressive pricing policies of the much larger Highland. The company faced bankruptcy.

Schulze and his team decided to survey Best Buy's customers on what appealed to them the most. The results were sobering. The average customer, especially women, disliked the shopping experience in a Best Buy Concept I store. Most women felt intimidated by the commissioned salespeople in the store and reported that they were often forced to buy higher-ticket items under the pretext that the product originally asked for was not in stock. Stung by the findings of its survey, Best Buy introduced its Concept II store in 1989—an everyday, low-price consumer electronics warehouse.

Becoming a Cost Leader: Concept II (1989–1994)

Although Concept I had helped to build skills in managing inventories, Concept II required a lot more. It was primarily a build strategy. Under this new strategy, all available merchandise was on display in the store. The backroom was eliminated. The company used a self-service, discount-style format with everyday low prices. There were no more commissions for the sales force. Salespeople were put on straight salary and were there only to help or advise customers when approached. The aim was to create a "no-pressure" shopping experience for the customer and grow revenue.

Best Buy's revenue grew from around $500,000 in 1989 to nearly $5 billion by 1994. It also expanded its market reach to include both male and female shoppers and its geographic reach to the entire upper Midwestern United States.

The other aim of Concept II was to trim by half the selling costs to compensate for the lower margins. This proved to be a challenge. Top management invited consultants in for the first time and revamped the company's inventory-management and logistics systems. The company eventually successfully trimmed its selling, general, and administrative expense ratio from 20.8 percent of sales in 1989 to 11.2 percent by the end of 1994. In fact, it became an industry leader in operational and logistical efficiency.

Despite its improved operational efficiency, profitability continued to get squeezed. Schulze felt it was time to change strategy yet again.

Attempting a Hybrid Approach: Concept III (1995–1998)

With Concept III, Best Buy sought to provide under a single roof both low-end commodity merchandise, such as video recorders, and higher-end products that still retained a lot of "myth," such as big-screen TVs and car stereos. The idea was to launch a hybrid store that, in addition to traditional commodity products, would carry higher-end merchandise with their better margins. Margins would also be helped by the sale of extended warranties for these high-priced products. The concerns with the new concept were many. Could the planned higher-end merchandise sit harmoniously with the low-end merchandise? Would customers get confused?

The company learned the virtues of trimming its product offerings at the low end. There had been a tendency under Concept II to match competitors, model for model, in every product category. This was stopped. As another first in its industry, Best Buy introduced the information kiosk: a touch-screen answer center containing product demonstrations and information on features and functions. The kiosks were expected to provide high levels of information on new products while keeping selling costs down. Over time, Best Buy learned that shoppers used these kiosks to learn more about new products but did not necessarily buy them in one of their stores. The company had to replace the kiosks with specialized departments for selling high-end products. Merchandising these new products was another learning experience.

The company also began selling extended warranties for the first time. Called Performance Service Plans, or PSPs, these warranties helped improve store margins; but top management was concerned that selling these plans might harm the "no-pressure" sales environment that the company had so carefully built under Concept II. Best Buy hired the Gallup polling company to do periodic surveys of its customers to ensure that being offered PSPs did not unduly pressure them.

The company overtook Circuit City in 1996 to become the largest consumer electronics retailer in the United States. Even though Concept III was largely a build strategy, it also had elements of leverage. It helped the company expand its geographic reach and start serving the needs of an entire family. Best Buy was fast becoming a national chain, serving the needs of both price-conscious customers and those looking for advanced products at a discount price. Concept IV was initiated to build the competencies needed to serve this new need.

Moving beyond Discrete Products: Concept IV (1998–2000)

The emergence of digital technology in the late 1990s forced Best Buy's top management to rethink its strategy yet again. Digital consumer electronics products—such as direct-broadcast satellite systems, digital cameras, DVD systems, cell phones, and high-definition television—were starting to make their way into homes. The new products generated a great deal of media hype and confusion among consumers. With Concept IV, Best Buy sought to be the place where people could learn about the latest digital products and decide what would best suit their specific needs.

Digital products were displayed creatively in a new "digital imaging area." Scanners and printers were connected to digital cameras, for example, and were actively demonstrated by sales staff. Customers could have their picture taken with a digital camera and get a copy from a printer or, alternatively, send it over the Internet to a friend or family member. The company also developed a Web-based distribution channel (bestbuy.com) to provide a seamless connection between the physical stores and the virtual one. Research could be done online; orders could be placed both online and in the store; delivery and returns could be at the store or at home, depending on the customer's preferences.

With the advent of the Concept IV store, Best Buy's retail strategy started to take a new focus. The traditional electronics and computer departments began giving way to more specialized departments for cell phones, satellite dishes, digital imaging, and home theater. Well-trained salespeople serviced the high-touch areas. Even though they were still noncommissioned, staff in the high-touch areas received a team bonus for extra sales. Their fixed salaries were also higher than the salary of the average Best Buy salesperson. And, because of their greater levels of expertise, they had better career opportunities, too.

In addition to having to cope with new product and technology launches during Concept IV, Best Buy saw a growing demand for services, such as providing customers with an Internet connection along with the sale of a PC. But, with the rise of digital products, shoppers needed service of a different level of expertise and complexity. First, they needed help in making the transition from analog to digital products. Second, they needed help in connecting all their different devices, be they analog or digital. Best Buy had become a company that had unique competencies in bundling consumer electronics products with associated services and in seamlessly blending the online experiences of customers with their in-store experiences.

Selling Solutions: Concept V (2001–2003)

This was both a build and leverage initiative. Introduced in 2001, this concept was aimed at keeping up with the rapid technological innovations in the consumer electronics and computer industries. In-store consultants handled complicated transactions and sold packages (product, services, warranty). For example, a customer might walk in to buy a digital camera ($999) and a camcorder ($499) and end up buying additional complementary products worth $2,198, accessories worth $607, extended warranties worth $250, and in-home installation and service worth $350, making a total purchase of more than double what the customer first intended. Best Buy had to build new skills in its sales team to sense and solve customer problems and not just satisfy customer wants.

The stores were made more modular. Store layouts could be reconfigured overnight, when necessary. This flexibility was considered necessary both for adapting to the changing needs of the customer and for matching the latest retailing innovations offered by competitors. For example, Best Buy was one of the first retailers to launch HDTV, with large numbers of products on display, high-quality demonstrations, and an HDTV focus in sales-staff training. When television programs offered in high-definition format did not materialize and the satellite companies cut the number of high definition channels from three to one, Best Buy scaled down its investments in HDTV and adapted its stores accordingly. However, there were also surprise hits like the TiVO, a digital device that could record from multiple TV channels simultaneously. This came "out of nowhere" to become an instant hit with customers. A modular store gave Best Buy the flexibility to shrink or expand its different departments at will.

The company also leveraged its vast retailing competencies to open smaller and multistoried inner-city stores in large cities on both coasts. This finally made the company a true national chain, with stores from New York City to Los Angeles, Minneapolis to Houston. It also ventured abroad for the first time by opening stores in Canada and acquiring Future Shop, the leading Canadian electronics merchant. The company continued to grow strongly; and, by 2003, it operated 679 stores. Gross margins climbed from 13.5 percent in 1997 to 25 percent in 2003.

Getting Closer to the Customer: Concept VII (2004–)

Brad Anderson became Best Buy's CEO in July 2002, taking over from its legendary founder, Dick Schulze. Anderson was impressed by Concept V's focus on solving customer problems and enhancing store flexibility. He wanted to extend this even further through a transformational initiative that he called Concept VII. There were many rationales for this new concept. The boundaries in the industry were blurring, with content providers and electronics vendors selling directly to end consumers. In parallel, new competitors had emerged with new business models that were much nimbler than Best Buy's. Mass discounters, led by Wal-Mart, had increased their share of the market to 21 percent; direct retailers held another 8 percent and were growing rapidly. The only way Best Buy could continue to be a leader was to control "the last 10 feet to the customer."

The approach Anderson chose required Best Buy to quantify the profitability of each of its customers. Best Buy's marketing team tried to discover why some customers were profitable and others were not. Using the insights from this analysis, it came up with five potentially profitable segments for the company. The new segments were defined more in terms of consumer needs and behaviors than demographic characteristics, as had been the case in the past. Small business owners and professionals became important new market segments for Best Buy.

The next challenge was to find ways to reengineer the customer experience and address the specific needs within each segment and its subsegments. New value propositions were formulated for each subsegment. Each value proposition had a well-thought-out store strategy, too. This meant tailoring product assortments, reviewing the 25,000 storekeeping units, or SKUs, to determine whether they were appropriate to a particular store, and adjusting the merchandise according to the income level and buying habits of local shoppers. A store-operating model was then defined to help implement the selected strategy.

Implementing this new strategy has been quite a challenge for Best Buy. The company first tested this idea in 32 of its stores. To make it a success, the company has had to train store employees to carry more of the responsibility for store-level merchandizing decisions. Customer-centricity has also meant empowerment of store employees. This has caused some frictions with executives in the company's headquarters who have had to share decision-making rights. However, they are still accountable for ensuring companywide standards and for overall system efficiency. Best Buy is, after all, a discount retailer; its name and yellow tag logo are reminders of this.

The results from the test stores were encouraging, with sales gains of 7 percent or higher. The company saw improvements in customer loyalty, employee retention, and market share. The members in Best Buy's Reward Zone, a customer loyalty program, grew to 7.2 million by 2006. By 2006, Best Buy had converted 300, or 40 percent, of U.S. Best Buy stores to the customer-centricity model, and it had rolled out the processes and human elements of the customer-centricity strategy to all of its stores.

The company finished fiscal year 2006 with revenue of $30.8 billion, a growth of 12 percent over the preceding year, with a 22 percent growth in earnings from continuing operations. Brad Anderson, the company's CEO, attributed this impressive profitable growth to customer-centricity.

New Build and Leverage Initiatives

> **Organizational capabilities.** Creating an organization that can balance the simultaneous needs of customers as well as store procurement and logistical efficiency has been a lingering challenge; empowering store employees and yet encouraging them to think about the health of the corporation has been another challenge for Best Buy.

The company planned to introduce by 2007 a single customer-centric operating model in all of its U.S. stores and corporate campus that would combine the best of its traditional, highly disciplined operating model with the more flexible, customer-centric model. Best Buy also embarked on a four-year program to transform its supply-chain and information technology systems. It seeks to build a simple infrastructure that is faster, cheaper, and more flexible.

Simultaneously, Best Buy has strengthened its human resource management systems, deploying employees to tasks suited to their strengths and providing store-based incentives. Individual incentives are still an anathema to the company. Retention rates have improved as a result.

Anderson sees this emerging organizational capability as one of Best Buy's key distinctive competencies for the future. Its competitors may be able to imitate Best Buy's customer-centric strategy on paper, but they will have a hard time executing against it without this organizational capability.

> **Services.** Best Buy has been steadily building its service capabilities. Its residential and commercial computer-support services business, offered under the name Geek Squad, employed 12,000 agents in 2006. The Geek Squad initially worked out of Best Buy stores. With the establishment of a central services depot in Memphis, called the Geek Squad City, Best Buy has built a platform to scale up its PC services business efficiently. The market for these services is estimated at $50 billion, offering another attractive growth opportunity for Best Buy.

> Best Buy also expanded its skills in home theater installation services through two small acquisitions in 2005. It had an in-house crew of 1,500 in 2006 to service the product sales made by its fast-expanding Magnolia Home Theaters—a store within a Best Buy store.

> **International expansion.** In a gutsy move, Best Buy finally leapt from its North American playground by acquiring in December 2006 a majority interest in Jiangsu Five Star Appliance. Jiangsu, China's fourth-largest appliance and consumer electronics retailer, operated 136 stores in that country and generated revenue of nearly $700 million. Best Buy paid $180 million for its controlling interest in that company. It also had plans to open its own store in Shanghai.

Reflecting on the Journey

As Figure 3.2 summarizes, Best Buy has progressively built and modified its competence platform from an early emphasis on operational excellence to complement it with modularity, flexibility, and customer-centricity. Correspondingly, its market reach has grown from Minnesota to all of North America and now to China, from male shoppers to the entire family, from cost-conscious shoppers to shoppers who care about product and service value. The various renewal strategies have reinforced each other. The company has changed dramatically in the past four decades, but it has not witnessed any revolutions. Best Buy has experienced gradual but continuous transformation under two different CEOs. Corporate renewal requires a sustained momentum that transcends top management transitions.

Summary

In continuous renewal, the firm is transformed over time but through a sustained sequence of leverage (leading to build) and build (leading to leverage) strategies.

Best Buy provides an interesting example of continuous renewal. It has transformed itself from relative obscurity to becoming the unquestioned industry leader in retailing consumer electronics in North America, with an eye on replicating that success in China. It has done so over four decades through six distinct renewal initiatives, each called a concept in the company's jargon.

Each concept has helped the company expand its market scope or grow its distinctive competencies. In addition, the momentum for each concept has come from the previous one, with a steadily accelerating pace. The various renewal strategies have reinforced each other. The company has sustained profitable growth over the past decade.

Top management has had the stamina and dedication to persist with this effort through changes in its own ranks.

CHAPTER 4

A Blended Approach

"Acquisitions are a great way to enhance and extend your business rapidly. But you cannot rely upon them. They may not be available at a price and time when you want them. Instead, I believe acquisitions should be used to supplement internal growth opportunities, not substitute for them."

—William (Bill) George, former chairman & CEO, Medtronic

The emphasis in the previous chapters was on organic growth. When the exploitation and expansion of a firm's market opportunities and distinctive competencies happen primarily through efforts internal to the firm, these are said to be *organic*. The firm can also *acquire* the market access and distinctive competencies that it needs, instead of developing them on its own; or partner with another firm to gain access to its markets and distinctive competencies, instead of purchasing these missing elements outright. These partnerships are popularly called *strategic alliances*.

Organic growth, acquisitions, and alliances are not strategies; instead, they are complementary means for implementing the four renewal strategies described previously in Chapter 2, "Renewal Strategies." One cannot assess the means without also examining the goal they seek to serve. Prior studies that have sought to evaluate the merits of mergers, acquisitions, alliances, or organic growth, without reference to the strategies that they are aimed at, miss this simple truth.

We devote the bulk of this chapter to how acquisitions and alliances can complement the role that organic growth plays in the continuous renewal of the firm. We also provide the example of Medtronic and show how it has blended organic growth, acquisitions, and alliances to generate spectacular and sustained profitable growth.

The Wrong Preoccupation

A question that seems to preoccupy managers is whether organic efforts internal to the firm, external acquisitions, or alliances are the preferred approach for driving profitable growth. Both scholars and consultants have examined this question, and the answer is mixed.

Impact of Acquisitions

The impact of acquisitions on firm performance has been studied extensively. The predominant finding is that mergers and acquisitions (M&As) do not create value for the acquiring company's shareholders in more than two-thirds of the cases. An example is a study done by the consulting firm KPMG International. It surveyed the 700 most expensive international M&A deals from 1996 to 1998 and concluded that only 17 percent of these deals had added value to the combined company, whereas 30 percent had had no impact whatsoever, and as many as 53 percent had actually destroyed value.[1]

However, there are also a few studies in support. For example, a recent study by the Boston Consulting Group (BCG) analyzed the long-term stock market performance of more than 700 large, publicly held U.S. companies over a 10-year period ending in 2002. It divided the sample firms into three clusters depending on their level of M&A activity. It found that the highly acquisitive group of companies had the highest median total shareholder return (TSR)—more than a full percentage point per year higher than the median TSR of companies that made few or no acquisitions.[2]

Impact of Strategic Alliances

The impact of strategic alliances on firm performance has been less well studied. The BCG provides one interesting finding.[3] Of the strategic alliances struck worldwide between 1988 and 2004, BCG points out that only about a third were winners. By winners, they mean that the alliance generated a positive announcement effect in the share prices of the participating companies of 4 percent or better. As with acquisitions, a majority of alliances, too, don't seem to add value for shareholders.

Alliance announcements that sought to build new competencies for the firm received the highest approval from the stock market. But these represented only 12 percent of all alliances.

Impact of Organic Growth

The story with organic growth is more positive. Investments in organic growth are typically measured by looking at research and development (R&D) expenses and capital expenditures. These are the two primary internal vehicles for driving growth.

The British government commissions a study each year to measure the impact of acquisitions and organic growth on the stock market performance of the top publicly listed companies in the United Kingdom.[4] For each company, the share price performance from the date of the largest single acquisition is compared with the *Financial Times* All-Share Index over the same period. More than two-thirds of the companies that had made a major acquisition underperformed the All-Share Index by nearly 40 percent. By contrast, investments in R&D and capital expenditures had a positive effect on shareholder returns.

Similar support comes from an academic study that looked at a sample of 134 U.S. companies with sizable R&D budgets and, after eliminating the effect of acquisitions, demonstrated that a higher R&D-to-sales ratio benefited the firm over the next decade through a higher rate of sales growth.[5] However, critics have argued that the payoffs from investments in R&D depend on the innovation context of the firm, which varies from industry to industry.

Making Sense of Claims and Counterclaims

The claims and counterclaims in the previous sections are hard to evaluate. There is little comparability across the studies. The samples chosen are different, the time windows vary, and the methodology is not the same.

In our own study, we looked at whether the financial performance of a firm was related to its acquisition intensity. Acquisition intensity (percent) was measured by dividing the sum total of all deal values over a five-year period by the sum total of firm revenue over the same five-year period. It is a measure of a firm's acquisition activity, adjusted for its size.

Firms that sustained profitable growth had on average an acquisition intensity of 10.5 percent, not the highest (Table 4.1). Firms that sustained growth only (and not profitability), in fact, had on average the highest acquisition intensity (14.4 percent).

We also looked at the impact of organic growth intensity on firm performance. Organic growth intensity (percent) was measured as the capital investment and R&D expenses that a firm incurs over a five-year period divided by its revenue over the same period.

Here again, firms that sustained profitable growth on average invested 10.1 percent of their revenue in R&D and capital expenditures (see Table 4.1), again not the highest. In fact, there was not much to distinguish the four performance categories on their organic growth intensity.

Table 4.1

Sustained Profitable Growth, Acquisition, and Organic Growth
Intensity

Performance Category	5 Year Average 2000-2004	
	Acquisition Intensity (percent)	Organic Growth Intensity (per cent)
Sustained Profitability and Growth	10.5	10.1
Sustained Growth only	14.4	12.4
Sustained Profitability only	5.7	9.8
Neither Growth Nor Profitability	4.8	8.9

Apart from pointing out that investment in both acquisitions and organic growth helps sustain profitable growth, our study does not show any particular advantage of either acquisitions or organic growth over the other in this endeavor. Both are necessary, but their magnitude is less important.

Comparing the relative merits of organic growth, acquisitions, and alliances is perhaps then the wrong preoccupation. What matters more is how each of these three means is deployed to execute the four renewal strategies described previously in Chapter 2.

Supporting the Transform Strategy

Transforming a firm through organic growth takes time and persistence. If a company seeks to transform itself more quickly, mega-acquisitions, combined with divestitures, are the preferred approach. The company literally has to buy its way into a new business and, on occasion, sell off its heritage if that can no longer fuel profitable growth.

Buying a New Identity

Consider the case of Vivendi Universal. In 1994, Jean-Marie Messier was hired by Générale Compagnie des Eaux, a vast international conglomerate with interests including water treatment, energy, construction, and telecommunications. Two years later, he became CEO at the age of 39 and launched a plan to steer the company into new growth markets. His vision was to turn this "boring" company, primarily a French water utility, into the world's preferred creator of entertainment, education, and personalized services to consumers anywhere, at any time, and across all distribution platforms and devices. The logic, given the huge economies of scale in producing digital information, whether as sound, vision, or the written word, was that a single company should do the whole thing—and that it had to be a giant. Because Messier wanted to grow faster than the competition, he went on an acquisition spree and spent $100 billion in five years.

In 2000, Messier merged his company with the Canadian beverage conglomerate Seagram, creating the world's second-largest media group. Hollywood's Universal Studios was acquired the same year for a price of $30 billion, and the entertainment assets of USA Networks were bought in 2001 for $10.5 billion. On paper, Messier had married content and distribution. The European pay-TV group Canal+ and French mobile phone group Cegetel would provide distribution platforms to sell Universal film and music properties. To many observers, however, Vivendi looked more like a muddled conglomerate. More worrisome, Vivendi had a colossal $19 billion debt.

The company had borrowed billions of dollars against the assets and steady cash flows of its utility business, Vivendi Environnement (VE). Messier then spun off VE in 2000, leaving Vivendi Universal with a 72.3 percent stake and saddling VE with huge debts. As Vivendi Universal's debts mounted and its liquidity problems intensified in 2002, the pressure grew for it to sell more of its VE stake to raise cash and allow it to deconsolidate VE's debt from its own balance sheet.

Then the Internet bubble burst, forcing Vivendi to report an $8.3 billion loss in March 2002 after revaluing assets acquired during the dot-com boom. This was followed by a $27 billion goodwill write-off in 2002. Vivendi also booked an additional $3.4 billion in financial provisions to cover losses on various investments, including $600 million in connection with its off-balance-sheet liabilities. The company's stock collapsed, and its credit rating was downgraded to junk status, which in turn increased the cost of its debt and finally led to its inability to make short-term debt interest payments. Messier was quickly ousted and replaced with a more conservative French CEO, Jean-René Fourtou.

One could argue that Vivendi had been caught in a market downdraft and was not entirely to blame for its market woes. One cannot blame Messier either. He had a grand vision, and we would be celebrating his genius if he had only had a few lucky breaks. The issue, however, is how much risk corporate leaders should take in pursuit of their transformational vision. Buying a new identity is expensive and risky. Remember the similar difficulties faced by Westinghouse and Monsanto in their efforts at transformation. Perhaps a better approach is to use M&As to buy a growth platform and then leverage it organically. This is precisely what Nokia did.

Acquiring a Platform for Transformation

The roots of Nokia go back to 1865 with the establishment of a forest industry enterprise in southwestern Finland. This business was merged in 1967 with Finnish Rubber Works Ltd. and Finnish Cable Works to form Nokia Corporation. Then early in the 1980s, Nokia strengthened its position in the telecommunications and consumer electronics markets through the acquisitions of Mobira, Salora, Televa, and Luxor of Sweden. In 1987, Nokia acquired the consumer electronics operations and part of the component business of the German Standard Elektrik Lorenz as well as the French consumer electronics company Oceanic. In 1987, Nokia also purchased the Swiss cable machinery company Maillefer. In the late 1980s, Nokia became the largest Scandinavian information technology company through the acquisition of Ericsson's data systems division. In 1989, Nokia conducted a significant expansion of its cable industry into continental Europe by acquiring the Dutch cable company NKF.

In 1992, the company felt the effects of a general slowdown in Europe. Furthermore, the Soviet Union, a valuable trading partner, was in poor economic shape. Nokia lost more than $200 million from 1991 to 1992. Then, in January 1992, Jorma Ollila became Nokia's new CEO. He soon decided to focus on two businesses with a future: (1) equipment and systems for fixed and mobile networks and (2) mobile phones. In the next few years, all other businesses were divested. Building on a few acquisitions, but also depending on its own R&D, Nokia has become arguably the world leader today in mobile phones, with a strong presence in 140 countries. The company has the highest market capitalization in Europe today and is also its strongest brand.

Acquisitions are not destinations, but starting points. As in the Nokia example, corporate leaders need to have a clear idea of what organic growth initiatives will follow the mega-acquisitions and divestitures in this transformational journey.

Supporting the Protect and Extend Strategy

Acquiring to Consolidate Industry Power

Acquisitions can help a protect and extend strategy by consolidating market power. Consider the mega-mergers in the oil or pharmaceutical industries, for example. Exxon's merger with Mobil and BP's merger with Amoco were directed at consolidating market power and eliminating wasteful redundancies. A similar situation encouraged the merger of Schweizerische Bankgesellschaft of Basel and Union Bank of Switzerland of Zurich to become UBS, the biggest banking organization in Switzerland and one of the top five worldwide. Glaxo's merger with Smith Kline Beecham and Ciba-Geigy's merger with Sandoz were aimed not only at these two goals but also at pooling the drug-discovery pipelines of these giants and rationalizing R&D spending.

An important consideration in acquisitions that support a protect and extend strategy is quick assimilation. Take the case of ISS, A/S (Integrated Service Solutions). It is a large service company based in Copenhagen, Denmark. Although probably best known for providing cleaning services, it performs numerous additional tasks, such as catering, property maintenance, and reception services. ISS presently employs more than 350,000 people in 46 countries. It unhesitatingly admits that its acquisitions will be absorbed quickly into the ISS fold. It has very clear rules for this integration:

> Immediate adoption of the ISS brand name.
> Immediate introduction of ISS's planning and financial control systems. These provide clear guidelines on how each activity within ISS is to be run. They also generate comparative data between the various operating units to assess effectiveness and to enhance learning across units.
> Retention only of members of the senior management team of the acquired company who subscribe to the preceding two rules.

Multiparty Alliances for Quick Execution

More and more companies are discovering the benefits of "open-market innovation," or mutually beneficial partnerships in R&D. The experience of Tetra Pak, one of the world's largest manufacturers of packaging systems for food products, illustrates the benefits of such an approach. At the beginning of the 1990s, Tetra Pak was attempting to develop a new type of food packaging that would challenge the leadership of metal cans and glass containers. Having tried to develop this technology in-house,

Tetra Pak realized that it did not have the right capabilities and decided to work with outside partners.

The venture eventually combined the expertise from three main sources:

> Traditional suppliers, such as those for papers and polymers, who helped Tetra Pak design the paperboard container that would resist high temperature and humidity .

> Tetra Pak's own research team, which developed new lamination techniques and the "form, fill, and seal" processes.

> New partners who were brought on board for a specific expertise. (For instance, a company specializing in sterilizing medical equipment was asked to help Tetra Pak find a way to sterilize the food inside the paperboard containers.)

By concentrating on the things it does best and sourcing ideas in areas in which it had less expertise, Tetra Pak was able to drastically reduce the time it took to develop and commercialize this breakthrough product. Tetra Recart has the potential to revolutionize the food packaging industry by enabling Tetra Pak customers to sterilize paperboard containers filled with liquid and soft food products. The package is also lighter, and its rectangular shape fits conveniently on retailers' shelves, increasing the number of units that can be displayed by as much as 50 percent over competing containers. Tetra Recart won the 2002 DuPont Diamond Award for innovation.

The Tetra Recart case is a good illustration of when to use multiple alliances.[6] Each of the Tetra Pak partners was a specialist in what it did and enjoyed large-scale economies. However, the specialization was also not directed at a specific product. Working

083 A Blended Approach

with these partners gave Tetra Pak the benefits of their expertise without the fear of a reciprocal transfer of its own product ideas. It was simultaneously able to protect and extend its core business.

Supporting the Build Strategy

A build renewal strategy is often hard to justify under the resource-allocation practices used in many corporations. There are typically two rationales for building a new competence: (1) how it can help strengthen the firm's competitive advantage in serving existing customers in current markets, and (2) how it can provide a growth platform to enter new markets in the future. The second is a hard sell. Visualizing all the opportunities that will be forthcoming is hard. Convincing top management of their commercial potential is even harder. In firms where the corporate leadership team either does not have the luxury of time to build a competence or is unwilling to absorb the risks of building a competence in-house, acquisitions and alliances might be the better approach.

Using Acquisitions to Accelerate the Building of Competencies

At Nestlé, acquisitions have been an important means for building new competencies for the company. The company was able to launch its confectionery, water, and pet food businesses primarily through mega-acquisitions.

For a leading food and beverage company, like Nestlé, adding water and pet food to its portfolio made sense. However, these were not businesses in which the company had core capabilities. By acquiring these capabilities and then leveraging them through Nestlé's international reach and distribution, the company has earned formidable leadership in both businesses. Nestlé would have found it difficult to achieve this global presence through an organic growth strategy.

Take the case of water. The bottled water segment now accounts for 9 percent of Nestlé's sales (or 8.8 billion Swiss francs in 2005) and for an even greater share of its profitability. Nestlé's former CEO, Helmut Maucher, was eager to diversify Nestlé's heavy dependence on food as the core product line in its corporate strategy. He took Nestlé into the water business in 1969 with the acquisition of 30 percent of the French Société des Eaux Minérales de Vittel (SGEMV). The company then acquired a controlling interest in SGEMV in 1992, and it further deepened its market presence by buying another French water company, Perrier, which owned a number of water brands, such as Perrier, Contrex, and Poland Springs in the United States—the world's largest water brand.

In 1997, the group gained leadership in the Italian market by acquiring a stake in the Italian brand San Pellegrino. It gained total ownership a few years later. This wide range of acquisitions gave Nestlé two competitive weapons: (1) local brands, such as Poland Springs, which were well adapted to local mass markets, and (2) premium brands, such as Perrier, San Pellegrino, and Vittel, which could be leveraged globally using Nestlé's market reach and logistics capabilities. By the end of 1997, Nestlé water was present on every continent.

But after it had created a new business platform through acquisitions, Nestlé moved on to an organic effort. Nestlé Pure Life is pure distilled water to which the company adds various types of salts to create distinct tastes. Pure Life has been a success, especially in developing countries. More recently, it has launched another one of its own brands called Aquarel, which uses a multispring concept to provide a low-mineral-content water that the whole family can drink. It also enables Nestlé to improve its use of invested capital by exploiting a portfolio of springs and filling plants.

As the Nestlé examples clearly show, when speed is of the essence and the desired capability is proven and well articulated by others, acquisitions are to be preferred over organic growth.

Complementary Alliances for Accessing Competencies

The Liechtenstein-based international tools company Hilti provides an instructive example here.[7] The company has focused on selling to professional power tool users in segments where it could maintain a leadership position. By 1996, Hilti was serving three distinct segments of the professional power tool market. Hilti believed it was servicing the top two segments effectively. The upper-segment customers were large construction companies working on big job sites. The middle-segment customers were involved in smaller building projects. In both segments of the market, customers were reached through the Hilti sales force. The one segment of the market that Hilti did not address effectively was the artisan segment. This segment consisted of professionals who worked on local job sites or dealt directly with private residential projects. In urban areas, a direct salesperson would try to locate these customers, but customers could only buy through Hilti Centers. Rural customers in this segment were not reached.

Hilti recognized that the market for professional power tools was changing. The artisan segment was becoming more attractive. More professionals were shopping at do-it-yourself (DIY) centers, and more retail consumers wanted high-quality tools. Hilti's competitors sold multiple brands and were already selling through indirect channels such as professional distributors. With its current strategy, Hilti had lower sales growth and margins in the artisan segment than most of its peers. At about this time, Hilti in France was approached by Saint-Gobain, a French building materials manufacturer and distributor. Saint-Gobain recognized the growth opportunity in the artisan segment and had created a new retail concept, "*La Plateforme du Batiment.*" Customers would purchase with a special card and be billed monthly. The company wanted to partner with ten key suppliers of building materials and wanted Hilti to be involved.

Hilti quickly agreed to a trial period in the first store. To protect its brand and operating margins, it demanded a shop within a shop, where Hilti-employed salespeople could sell directly to the customers visiting the Saint-Gobain stores. It also negotiated a preferential margin arrangement. Saint-Gobain agreed to both requests because of the strong effect that the Hilti brand would have in pulling customers to these new stores. The successful trial resulted in the retail concept being rolled out to new La Plateforme stores in France and brought the additional opportunity to participate in Saint-Gobain's international expansion. In 1999, Home Depot approached Hilti to implement a similar shop-in-shop concept in its 800 U.S. stores.

Even though the capability that the firm seeks to build may be well articulated and in the form of an asset—like the La Plateforme stores that Saint-Gobain offered Hilti—if this asset cannot be either fully utilized by the buyer or will need continuous development, alliance might be the better option.

Using Learning Alliances as a Step to Acquisition

Cisco Systems Inc., the premier provider of networking solutions in the world, is a case in point. Given the technological and commercial uncertainties around new technologies, Cisco has chosen not to build them in-house. Instead, it first engages in alliances with start-up companies that are interested in building these technologies. It typically takes a minority equity stake and, through its seat on the board of the start-up, assesses the growing worth of the technology under development. This privileged information then allows Cisco to acquire the company at the right time and at the right price.

Cisco acquired more than 36 companies from 1993 to 2003. This added capability helped the company grow its sales during that period by a compound annual rate of 36 percent. One of the reasons for Cisco's relative success in integrating so many acquisitions was that it targeted mostly small start-ups in a growing phase. Leveraging their capabilities through its well-oiled distribution channel, Cisco was then able to boost sales of acquired companies by bundling their products with others in Cisco's portfolio to offer a comprehensive range of networking solutions for clients.

It is important to recognize that Cisco had one senior vice president in charge of M&As, strategic alliances, and technology incubation. He and his team of vice presidents were able to systematically assess whether a competence could be built in-house within the desired time frame; and assess the risks that the company was willing to take. If not, were there target companies that had technology that was critical to Cisco's core products? If there was the possibility of immediately leveraging this technology, the target was quickly acquired. However, Cisco also recognized that less well articulated the capabilities that were being sought, the better alliances were for a build strategy. Cisco worried about losing the know-how and skills that the employees of its partner companies could bring. However, once a trusting relationship was established with these partner compaines, they were slowly acquired.[8]

Supporting the Leverage Strategy

Using Acquisitions to Leverage Available Competencies

Acquisitions can also be used to leverage a firm's competencies, but it is rare to buy just new market access. The target brings its own competencies, which, if well managed, can further strengthen the acquirer's core. Acquisitions, by creating tensions and clashes with existing routines, may break rigidities in acquiring firms and foster learning.

Consider, for example, the case of Best Buy. As previously described, the company had grown organically during its first 35 years. Then, in 2001, it made several acquisitions. The first, Musicland, turned out to be a flop, and the business was eventually divested in 2003. However, the later acquisition of Magnolia Hi-Fi and Future Shop turned out to be great for leverage. The purchases of Magnolia Hi-Fi, a West Coast consumer electronics chain, gave Best Buy access to the high-end segment of the industry. More recently, Magnolia has been integrated as a shop within a shop in close to 300 Best Buy stores. This allows the company to leverage many of its strengths, while still retaining Magnolia's separate identity and the new market segments that it allows Best Buy to enter.

In parallel, Best Buy expanded internationally by purchasing Future Shop, the leading Canadian electronics merchant (with a 16 percent market share and the number-one retail Web store in Canada). Future Shop was positioned toward a more upscale market segment and shared less than 55 percent of its product assortment with Best Buy. At one level, this was a simple geographic expansion. Best Buy figured that it was a lot easier to enter Canada by acquiring the leading discount retailer of consumer electronics in that country. In a few places in Canada where Best Buy had tried to expand organically, however, the company found that the Best Buy stores and Future Shop were only helping and not cannibalizing each other's sales. Future Shop was drawing a slightly upscale customer segment. Instead of retiring that brand, Best Buy has chosen to hold on to it for possible future leverage in other geographies, including the United Sates. In 2006, Best Buy had 119 Future Shops and 44 Best Buy stores in Canada.

Using Alliances to Reach New Markets

Using alliances for leverage is a popular option. The case of Corning Flint Glass is an excellent example of how this can be done. The company specializes in four main areas: (1) specialty materials such as ophthalmic glass; (2) communications equipment, such as optical fiber; (3) laboratory equipment, such as lighting; and (4) consumer products, such as Pyrex ovenware.

Corning has formed more than 40 joint ventures (complementary alliances) for leveraging its distinctive competencies in these four areas. This helps the company find new opportunities for its technologies much quicker than an internal effort would allow. However, the company insists on being fully involved with all of its joint ventures. It does not simply license its products to another company. For example, when Corning undertook an alliance with Asahi Glass, a company that supplies glass to the Japanese auto market, Corning insisted on getting market information back from Asahi so that its managers could begin learning about the Japanese market. This knowledge has helped Corning launch other ventures. A leverage strategy, if well executed, not only brings new markets to the firm but also new capabilities.

Multiparty Alliances for Build and Leverage

Multiparty alliances are becoming a popular way to enter new market space and to build new competencies.[9] For example, even Boeing—a traditionally vertically integrated firm—has begun to mirror the alliance strategy of its arch-competitor Airbus by picking more than 100 partners to work on its 787 aircraft.

Companies in a number of industries, such as pharmaceuticals, medical devices, aerospace, and information and communications, are increasingly using external networks to build missing competencies or to enter new markets. There is a lot of uncertainty in these industries as to which competencies, especially technology platforms, will be the winners in the future. Building new competencies is both expensive and risky, as is entry into new markets in emerging economies. Besides, competencies can become obsolete very quickly. Therefore, partnering and virtual networks are increasingly important.

The drug giant Eli Lilly calls its new approach "discovery without walls." The company's "find it" team—composed of more than 20 in-house research scientists—and its "get it" team work side by side to move quickly on the opportunities that they discover. These two teams review up to 1,500 opportunities each year, sign 350 confidentiality agreements, and complete around 40 partnership agreements. Finally, the "create value" group is the alliance management team. Its sole focus is managing the relationship between Lilly and its several dozen partners.

Another example is Procter & Gamble's (P&G) new connect and develop strategy.[10] When A. G. Lafley was appointed P&G's CEO in 2000, he realized that the company could not spend more and more on R&D for less and less payoff. He challenged the organization to reinvent the company's innovation business model by acquiring 50 percent of innovations from outside the company. Connect and develop emerged as a response to that challenge. P&G soon realized that for every P&G researcher there were 200 scientists or engineers elsewhere in the world who were just as good, so a total of 1.5 million people outside whose talents P&G could potentially use. It created an extended R&D organization connecting its own 7,500 researchers and engineers with this vast external pool through a permeable boundary. By 2005, more than 35 percent of P&G's new products had elements that originated outside the company, up from 15 percent in 2000. Its R&D productivity had increased by nearly 60 percent, and its innovation success rate more than doubled, while the cost of innovation had fallen.

A network structure, however, is advantageous only if the firm can maintain a central role within it. Consider a company like Cisco. It outsources some of its product development to partner companies. However, it always retains control, including the right to acquire its partners at a future date. A firm can be a central player only if it continues to excel either in the market access that it provides or in a capability that is key to adding value in its industry.

The much-vaunted networking ability of Nike, for example, centers on its ability to manage its brand and design. The challenge for corporate leaders is to continuously ensure this centrality when reviewing the firm's alliance strategies. They must also put in place processes that bind its partners to the firm. Boeing, for example, holds a partners "council meeting" every six weeks for this purpose and controls the data network through which its global partners communicate with each other. It is the central player in its network.

A Blended Approach to Spurring Continuous Renewal

As the previous examples richly illustrate, acquisitions and alliances can complement organic growth in supporting a firm's renewal strategies. How these are managed will depend on the strategy being supported.

Managing Acquisitions

Acquisitions can support all four renewal strategies—transform, build, leverage, and protect and extend—but are particularly useful in support of a transformation strategy (see Figure 4.1). Acquisitions are very helpful in supporting a build or leverage strategy, as well. Here , success depends on having a well-thought-out organic growth effort to follow. Finally, acquisitions can also help a protect and extend strategy, consolidating a firm's presence in its industry.

Although acquisitions are useful for spurring growth, they have to be looked at as part of a well-thought-out strategy and not just as a financial exercise. The huge premiums paid for acquisitions, averaging around 30 percent, cannot be recovered magically through productivity improvements and synergies that are brought to the target by the acquirer. A common failing is to squeeze the target for enhanced profitability. The logic is that this is required to pay for the lavish premiums that were paid in its acquisition. However, this can have the perverse effect of damaging the very capabilities for which the acquisition was made in the first place.

Depending on whether an acquisition is being made as part of a protect and extend, build, leverage, or transform growth strategy, integration of the target will differ.[11] On one hand, in acquisitions aimed at transforming the firm, the target is best left alone with little effort to integrate it with the core business. On the other hand, in acquisitions that support a protect and extend strategy, the target is best absorbed and quickly integrated with the core. Build and leverage strategies may require a hybrid approach, where the target is integrated progressively to exploit all potential synergies.

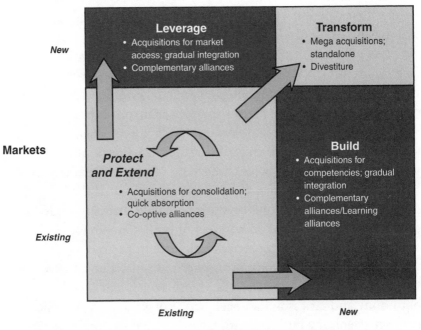

Figure 4.1
Role of acquisitions and alliances in corporate renewal.

Managing Strategic Alliances

Markets do not always have to be owned (either through internal development or acquisitions) for them to present a growth opportunity for the firm, and competencies do not have to be owned to become a source of competitive advantage. They can also be accessed through an alliance. Alliances are very useful in support of a leverage or build strategy. They are also used more routinely to protect and extend the core business. However, they are less useful to transform a business. If a firm is seeking to move away from its legacy, partnering with another offers no particular advantage. If it is the partner who brings both access to the new market that is being sought and the missing competencies, the firm has no influence in this relationship.

As with acquisitions, not all strategic alliances are the same (see Figure 4.1).[12] When a firm partners with another by pooling its resources to derive economies of scale or limit its risk, it is in a co-optive alliance. Only part of the firm is involved in the relationship—for example, sales or manufacturing—with the rest operating at arm's length from its partner. Co-optive alliances are well suited to serve a protect and extend strategy. The alliance between Intel and Microsoft to create what is called the Wintel platform is an example of a co-optive alliance that is intended to protect and extend the core business of both companies.

The Sony Ericsson co-optive alliance in the mobile telephony handsets business is another example. The alliance now has a combined market share of close to 10 percent. Previously, both Sony and Ericsson had been active players in the mobile handset telephony business without being able to dominate this segment, in which giants such as Nokia, Motorola, and Samsung were clearly leading.

When the motive is to leverage or build, there needs to be a deeper commitment. What the firm needs is more durable access to the complementary strengths, either in new market access or in new distinctive competencies that the partner has. The two partners have to work closely with each other because they control only part of the value chain. Such an association is called a complementary alliance. The alliance between Canon and Hewlett-Packard (HP) is one such. Canon and HP have for a long time had a successful strategic alliance on computer printers. All the printers are made by Canon, which also does all the R&D and product development. The printers are then sold by Hewlett-Packard under the HP brand. Thus, there is a clear division of labor between the two companies. Each sticks to its designated domain—no printer is manufactured by HP, and no printer is sold by Canon.

A build strategy may also be helped by a learning alliance such as the one between General Motors and Toyota on their New United Motor Manufacturing Inc. (NUMMI) project. The plant produces small cars for both Toyota and General Motors (Chevrolet). For General Motors, the major learning goal was access to Toyota's manufacturing and quality management processes. For Toyota, the learning goal was how to develop marketable products in the United States. In hindsight, the actual learning might not have been equally split. Toyota has excelled in penetrating the U.S. market and has introduced, on its own, an impressive number of car models that have captured major market share in the United States. General Motors, by contrast, has struggled to keep up with Toyota's quality and manufacturing methods, even though it has learned a lot through the NUMMI alliance.

A Blended Approach

There is a recurring theme in the examples that we have narrated so far. Acquisitions, alliances, and organic growth are not contending but complementary means of realizing a firm's renewal agenda. It is the job of the corporate leader to ensure that there is a broad template for coordinating the three, using each appropriately and coordinating them for maximum effect. We would like to present the Medtronic story next. Here is a company that has done a superb job of blending organic growth, acquisitions, and alliances in generating an enviable record of sustained profitable growth.

An Exemplar: Medtronic

Medtronic, an $11.3 billion medical appliances company in 2006, has increased its revenue on average by more than 15 percent each year, and it has earned on average more than 16 percent return on capital employed (ROCE) over the past five years. Medtronic's success has come primarily from organic growth, but acquisitions and alliances have provided important platforms (see text boxes in the figure) to drive this growth (see Figure 4.2).

The company has diversified its market presence over the years to provide a range of products, including those used in the treatment of cardiac arrhythmias, blood oxygenators and other equipment for cardiac surgery, tissue and mechanical heart valves, stents for vascular medicine and surgery, implantable devices to treat neurological problems such as Parkinson's disease, and more recently, fusion systems and other treatments for spinal deformities, bone fractures and degenerative discs, medical appliances for ENT (ear, nose and throat) care, the treatment of diabetes, and gastroenterology and urology problems. Each Medtronic product is aimed at a chronic disease, and the company is committed to improving the care and quality of life of patients with these diseases.

Arthur (Art) Collins, Jr., the company' chairman and CEO, notes that the excitement surrounding Medtronic goes beyond its superb financial performance. He emphasizes that the company is in the business of improving and saving lives.

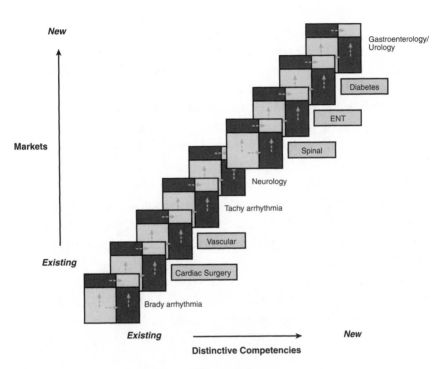

Figure 4.2
Blending M&A and organic growth at Medtronic.

Making Acquisitions to Set Up New Growth Platforms

Build or transform strategies are riskier than the other two renewal strategies. As noted previously, justifying the building of a new competence, especially to compete in a market that is also new to the firm, is hard to do. In cases like this, resorting to acquisitions may help. The competence acquired is tangible and proven and is already being applied to serve a market—hopefully close to the one that the firm is after. The challenge for the firm is to absorb this competence and start applying it to the market needs that it has identified without killing off the positive cash flows that the acquired competence is able to generate.

The Medtronic story provides a great example of how to do it.[13] The company's visioning exercises over the years clearly showed the need first to expand its capabilities in cardiac disease management beyond pacemakers into valves, stents, and cardiac surgery equipment; and then to extend them to other chronic diseases. Each of these diversifications was first helped by a platform that was acquired. It would have been too time-consuming and risky for Medtronic to attempt to build these competencies on its own. Although there was also a good overlap between the markets served by these targets and the ones that Medtronic was interested in, the positive cash flows that each target generated post-acquisition made it easier to justify these build/transform actions.

Medtronic first began making acquisitions when Win Wallin took over as CEO in the mid-1980s. These continued under his two successors, Bill George and Art Collins. Medtronic made more than 30 acquisitions from 1986 to 2006, primarily to enter the cardiac surgery, vascular, ENT, diabetes, spinal-care businesses (see the text boxes in Figure 4.2), but also to strengthen its cardiac rhythm management (CRM), neurology, gastroenterology, and urology businesses.

Medtronic only engages in acquisitions if it has a good understanding of at least one facet of the target: customers, technology, or distribution. The target has to fit Medtronic's strategy and either have a leading position in its market or offer Medtronic the capabilities that it needs to strengthen its business in that market. Instead of being swayed by the emotions of a deal, Collins insists that Medtronic considers only targets that add strategic value:

By and large, we operate in highly underpenetrated markets, where only a percentage of the individuals who could benefit from the therapy have received it.

Entry into the diabetes market is a good example. The company has leveraged its acquisitions and offers insulin pumps and continuous glucose monitoring to chronic diabetes patients. The company has barely penetrated a quarter of this market, even though it is the industry leader. Growth for Medtronic means growing an underpenetrated market more than fighting competitors for market share in a maturing market, even though the company is very successful at that, too.

However, the company did not see acquisitions as the primary vehicle for growth; instead, it used them as a supplement to support organic growth. George explained the reasoning:

> *Predicting the timing and availability of acquisition candidates is extremely difficult. If you are counting on them for growth, there is a real risk of making the wrong acquisition or paying too much for it. If acquisitions become the dominant growth vehicle, operating problems with them will eventually squeeze out funds required for long-term internal growth programs.*

The targets that the company acquired had their own culture and mission, and Medtronic realized that it was very hard to get the hearts and minds of the acquirer and target aligned. Top management at Medtronic reasoned that it would only be able to retain the skilled talent that it was acquiring by ensuring that the target business and its employees would have even more opportunities for profitable growth within the Medtronic family than as a standalone company. Organic growth subsequent to an acquisition was important for this reason, too.

Using Organic Growth as a Stabilizing Force

Hand in hand with its acquisitions, Medtronic has also invested a great deal in its efforts at organic growth. R&D spending at the company has averaged more than 10 percent per year. At any given time, Medtronic works on five generations of products and has consciously sought to generate approximately two-thirds of its revenue from products introduced just 24 months earlier. The cycle time for developing products has also been dramatically cut by two-thirds, from 48 to 16 months.

Under the company's Quest program, all employees worldwide are encouraged to submit proposals for new products, technologies, and processes. Accepted proposals receive seed money up to an annual maximum of $50,000. Quest forms a conduit for ideas that typically do not survive the gauntlet of annual planning and budgeting activities. A great example of a Quest project is the super-low-cost pacemaker initiated by a bunch of Medtronic engineers who sought to manufacture a reliable pacemaker at one-sixth of the prevailing cost. This project subsequently became the inspiration for the innovative Champion pacemaker that was successfully launched in China. It also forced Medtronic to take a harder look at its design and manufacturing processes and optimize them for cost savings across the company's entire product line.

Using Strategic Alliances to Access New Competencies

Medtronic looks to strategic alliances to fill the gaps in its technology portfolio. It has numerous strategic alliances with universities, research laboratories, and smaller firms. It has also made several deals out of the public eye annually, primarily to acquire technology or intellectual property. Its minority stake gives Medtronic the first right to acquire new intellectual property and a board seat from which it can monitor the progress of the new technology. The company also has a number of key alliances (Microsoft, Dell, Cisco, and IBM) in pursuit of its Internet-based strategies.

The company has sought to integrate its implantable devices with sensor technology and, using information and communication media, has linked patients and physicians through its Patient Management Network. Perhaps one of Medtronic's most ambitious and innovative projects is to transmit data via the Internet to a clinic from devices implanted in patients. Doctors can access information never seen before about their patients' hearts via a secure Web browser. The first product launched under this project was the Chronicle implantable heart-failure monitor.

Other examples include Medtronic's partnerships with drug companies such as Abbott Labs, for its drug-coated stents, and Novartis, for delivering small amounts of bacinfen (that company's potent drug for relieving severe spasticity) via a Medtronic pump. Collaboration helps Medtronic push the envelope on new approaches to patient care.
Collins notes:

> *We are seeing convergence of biotechnology and biologics with medical devices, and of diagnostics with in-vivo therapy. This convergence is transforming patient care and is creating exciting opportunities for the company.*

An example is the company's joint venture, MG Biotherapeutics, with Genzyme, a leading biotechnology company, aimed at accelerating the development of new treatments for intractable forms of cardiovascular disease.

The Never-Ending Quest for Continuous Renewal

Although much has been achieved, Glen Nelson, Medtronic's retired vice chairman and its long-time technology champion, cautions that the challenge in going forward is to draw a fine line between existing and new technologies:

> *It is going to require a really thoughtful effort to leverage the current technologies and those that are coming in the future at an increasingly faster rate. We may need to cannibalize some of our own products and make dramatic, and sometimes painful, changes. At the same time, we will have to be good stewards of our resources and those of our partners and customers. Some of the technology that we'll ultimately use may be too far in the future for us to develop at this point in time. Drawing a fine line between what we do and don't do, and paying careful attention to how rapidly we adopt new technologies and business models, will, to a large extent, determine our success.*

Collins and his executive team are mindful of this challenge. By not relying solely on in-house development and organic growth, the company has successfully managed the risks in its renewal. It provides a very good example of how a blend of organic growth, acquisitions, and alliances can be a potent combination to execute a company's renewal strategies. In the six decades since its founding in 1949, the company has renewed itself continuously, diversifying its competence base and entering multiple market segments covering most major chronic disease states with the possible exception of cancer. Financial performance has followed. It has successfully sustained profitable growth.

Summary

Organic growth, acquisitions, and alliances are not strategies; instead, they are complementary means for implementing the four renewal strategies that were described in Chapter 2. There is no evidence that one is superior to the other in driving profitable growth. All are necessary, and their importance depends on the strategy for which they are deployed.

Acquisitions are particularly useful in support of a transformation strategy. The target is best left alone with little effort to integrate it with the core business. Alliances are less useful to transform a business.

Acquisitions can also help a protect and extend strategy, consolidating a firm's presence in its industry. The target is best absorbed and quickly integrated with the core. Alliances are used more routinely to protect and extend the core business. When a firm partners with another by pooling its resources to derive economies of scale or limit its risk, it is in a co-optive alliance. Co-optive alliances are well suited to serve a protect and extend strategy.

Acquisitions are helpful in supporting a build or leverage strategy, but success depends on having a well-thought-out organic growth effort to follow. The target should be integrated progressively to exploit all potential synergies.

Alliances are useful in support of leverage or build strategy. When the motive is to leverage or build, there needs to be a deeper commitment. What the firm needs is more durable access to the complementary strengths, either in new market access or in new distinctive competencies that the partner has. Such an association is called a *complementary alliance*. A build strategy may also be helped by a learning alliance.

A company such as Medtronic, which has sustained profitable growth by managing its continuous renewal with a clever blend of acquisitions and alliances to access new capabilities and markets but then built and leveraged these platforms through organic growth, offers a good example of how a blended approach can help sustain profitable growth.

PART II
Execution

CHAPTER 5

The Entrepreneur-Manager

"Companies need people who can take an idea, believe in it, and bring it to fruition against the odds."

—Camille Pagano, former senior executive vice president at Nestlé

In the first part of this book, we discussed the four renewal strategies that a firm needs to sustain profitable growth. Each can be supported by a blend of organic growth, acquisitions, and alliances. As you also saw in Chapter 4, "A Blended Approach," the mode of acquisition or alliance, and how it is executed, varies with the renewal strategy being supported. In Part II, we focus on executing organic growth.

Organic growth requires both a top-down and bottom-up effort (see Figure 5.1). Top management sets the broad vision for the firm and specifies the scope and pace of renewal. This is based on the assessment of the rate at which the firm's markets are maturing and its competence platforms losing their distinction, and also on its vision for where the firm should be headed in terms of new markets and competencies and how quickly.

Given this broad directive, senior executives, with the help of staff experts, define the renewal agenda for their organizational units, specifying the relative emphasis on protect and extend, leverage, build, and transform goals (and whether acquisitions and alliances will be used to serve these goals). For the goals targeted for organic growth, the firm's business and functional managers are invited to propose strategies. They shape these strategies in conjunction with senior management and take responsibility for their implementation.

However, a frequent problem is that the business and functional managers entrusted with the responsibility for shaping and implementing renewal strategies also have to deliver short-term results. Their priority is to exploit current markets and competencies rather than explore for new markets and competencies. In a sense, this is natural. As we discussed in Chapter 2, "Renewal Strategies," protect and extend is clearly an important renewal strategy. Realistically, this is the strategy to which a firm will allocate the bulk of its resources. The firm's short-term performance depends heavily on it. As we also showed in Chapter 3, "Continuous Renewal," however, sustaining profitable growth requires an emphasis on continuous renewal. The firm has to look beyond protect and extend to the strategies of leverage, build, and transform. These should not be neglected.

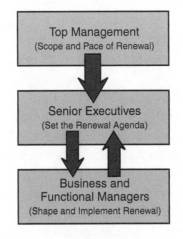

Figure 5.1
The strategy process.

Renewal also suffers because the personal qualities, skills, and experiences needed to manage leverage, build, and transform strategies are in short supply. As Nestlé's Chairman and CEO, Peter Brabeck-Letmathe, notes:

> *Many managers in large institutions have been trained to keep things running as they have been. They have learned to comply with an enormous number of detailed procedures and systems. They were taught by experience that they are better off following the expected and accepted tracks of routine rather than venturing out into the new and unexpected.*

Continuous renewal requires venturing out into the new and unexpected. In a survey conducted by the American Management Association, responding managers were asked to rank the competence of their firm's managerial corps on 27 conceptual, communication, effectiveness, and interpersonal skills. Key entrepreneurial skills—such as identifying opportunities for innovation, networking within and outside the organization, and working with diverse people and cultures—were ranked way down on that list. Managers entrusted with implementing renewal strategies, no matter where they are in an organization, are lacking in entrepreneurial skills. This hurts continuous renewal.

We need a dedicated and special kind of manager to execute the leverage, build, and transform strategies. Earlier, we referred to this individual as an entrepreneur-manager, a hybrid between an external entrepreneur and a good operating manager—having the external focus and risk-taking ability of the former and the discipline around delivery of the latter. Entrepreneur-manager is a label that we have coined. It does not exist in any of the organizations that we know. We use the hyphenated label intentionally to highlight what managers who drive renewal initiatives must have—entrepreneurial skills, to complement the operational skills that most of them bring.

In this chapter, we profile the desired qualities in an entrepreneur-manager (see Table 5.1). We have compiled this based on the experiences of Nestlé, Dow Chemical, Hewlett-Packard, and Ericsson in implementing renewal strategies (see box).

Table 5.1
Profile of an Entrepreneur-Manager

Skills
___

> See the big picture and shape strategy
> Communicate and market the strategy
> Manage stakeholders, gain support, and mobilize resources
> Assemble and motivate a team of experts

Personal Traits
___

> Propensity to take risks
> Passion & inner fire
> Action orientation
> Self confidence

Professional Traits
___

> Established track record—buys freedom and trust.
> Long tenure and varied experience—helps with networking

___

Five Renewal Strategies

Nestlé LC1[1]—Since the early 1990s, the Nestlé Research Center in Lausanne, Switzerland, has been working on the probiotic properties of a group of cultures called *Lactobacillus acidophilus,* referred to internally as LA-1. James Gallagher, head of the company's flagging yogurt business, saw in the LA-1 culture the opportunity to make yogurt a functional food and thus transform his business. This was a *build* strategy that has seen mixed success. It has since led to the creation of functional foods as an important growth platform for Nestlé.

Nespresso[2]—The Nespresso system consists of individually portioned aluminum capsules containing roast and ground coffee made for use in specially designed coffee machines. Nestlé holds patents for the capsules and machines but has licensed production of the machines to manufacturers and makes money solely off the capsules. In 1988, Yannick Lang,[3] an outsider from Philip Morris, was recruited to put this venture on a firm commercial footing. Lang had a reputation for creativity, having successfully built the Marlboro Classics clothing line. He retargeted the market

continues

continued

for Nespresso to the in-home user and built a direct channel and a separate brand identity. When he left in 1997 to pursue another career opportunity within Nestlé, Nespresso had grown to a 100 million Swiss francs business. Nespresso was a *transform* strategy that has since succeeded big.

Ericsson Cellular Transmission Systems (CTS)[4]—This project sought to provide a cheaper and more flexible system for mobile telecommunications operators. Ericsson's top management brought in Tsviatko Ganev, a mid-level executive who had worked in the company's component division, to lead this difficult project. After a few false starts, he was able to develop and market innovative solutions to Ericsson's problems related to the fixed-transmission component of its mobile cellular network. CTS is a key platform on which Ericsson has established its global leadership in mobile network systems. CTS was a *build* strategy that succeeded.

e-epoxy at Dow Chemical[5]—In 1999, Ian Telford worked in the Epoxy Products and Intermediates (EP&I) division of Dow Chemical, as its commercial director for Europe. Recognizing both the threat and opportunity that the Internet presented for Dow's epoxy products, Telford developed the idea of e-epoxy.com, an Internet site for purchasing epoxy from Dow at low price points. By late 2002, the revenues were still small, but the business was EBIT positive. It was expected that the venture would pay itself off in just over two years. Not only was the project a financial success, but it also established an important Internet platform for Dow Chemical. Dow's e-epoxy was a *build* strategy that was successful as a project but has since been terminated. The company has built on this experience to launch other more effective e-channels.

Hewlett-Packard's e-services[6]—In April 1998, a new business unit was formed at Hewlett-Packard, centering on utilizing the emerging Internet, and Nick Earle was appointed chief marketing officer. Earle believed that HP had ignored the Internet for long and relished the opportunity to help the company redirect its efforts. By January 1999, Earle's team had concluded that computing would become a continuum of brokered applications, and thus HP must serve these applications. The new products that would serve these needs were known collectively as "e-services." In November 1999, new CEO Carly Fiorina created a new business unit for e-services. The unit was charged to position HP at the center of new growth markets and catalyze change within HP. Soon after it was founded, many Internet stocks crumbled, and HP's investments foundered. In the summer of 2000, Earle left HP, and his second-in-command took over. The e-services unit lasted only another six months after Earle's departure. HP's e-services was a *leverage* strategy that failed to meet its goals and has since been terminated.

Skills of an Entrepreneur-Manager

See the Big Picture and Shape Strategy

Entrepreneur-managers are always loyal to the company's vision. Unlike external entrepreneurs, they do not march to their own drum. Each of the five ventures we have described had a business proposition that was anchored in the corporate strategy of the firm. For example, LC1 was aimed at building a new competence platform for Nestlé in functional foods; e-services at HP was aimed at leveraging HP's strengths in products into services; and the e-channel at Dow Chemical was aimed at building a new low-cost channel for the company.

Within this guiding vision, however, the entrepreneur-manager finds the freedom to develop strategies that can help in the firm's renewal. These are not just brilliant technical or commercial ideas but are instead a complete business proposition. As Peter Brabeck-Letmathe puts it: "Functional thinking keeps people from seeing business solutions." The entrepreneur-manager must have the mindset of a strategist—the ability to see the total business value of the venture that he manages.

Consider the following from HP. In 1998, Ann Livermore, then head of HP software and support, joined forces with HP's UNIX computer chief to create Enterprise Computing, the $35 billion business-to-business part of HP. Livermore appointed Nick Earle as chief marketing officer. Earle was frustrated by HP's reluctance to embrace the Internet. Within the broad vision of Enterprise Computing, he saw an opportunity to position HP in the Internet space. Earle recalled:

> *Nobody had anything to do with the Internet at HP. Strategy formulation was a product-centric process. By definition, every product was perfect because it performed to data-sheet specifications. But there was no process for strategizing in the*

*white space between the products. We realized that all we were
doing was trying to connect the dots among the most complicated
product portfolio out there. We had to leapfrog. It's going to
become a world of services. Computing is going to brokered
applications. It will be divided into subtasks, and the Internet
will become a big-task broker. Suppliers and customers will bid
on transactions. We called this "e-services."*

E-services was not just a technical or commercial idea, even
though it required technical breakthroughs and creative
commercial approaches; it was a new business proposition—
positioning HP as a service company and not a product company.
Although the e-services strategy eventually died at HP, it is a
good illustration of how an entrepreneur-manager has to be aware
of the firm's external business context and come up with new
business propositions for renewing the firm.

Formulating a new business proposition must also follow
another discipline: prudent risk management. Entrepreneur-
managers manage their ventures by anchoring them either in a
firm's distinctive competencies or in a market opportunity that the
firm dominates (see Figure 5.2). Although it may be impossible
for entrepreneur-managers to predict the future shape of an
industry, it is typically easier for them to see some broad trends
and identify new business opportunities before others do. Instead
of betting on these trends, the entrepreneur-manager investigates
them through careful experimentation, without committing new
resources to the market opportunity but by first leveraging the
available resources and skills of the firm.

Similarly, the entrepreneur-manager does not build a
new competence platform in anticipation of a future market
opportunity but instead erects these platforms in steps, serving
the firm's established markets first. This ability to be simultaneously focused on the future and anchored in either the firm's

current competencies or its already established markets allows the entrepreneur-manager to manage risks better. External entrepreneurs, by contrast, have neither an established market nor a proven competence to anchor their ventures. They *have* to be more risk seeking.

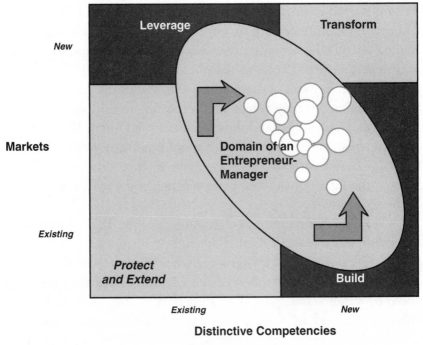

Figure 5.2
The domain of an entrepreneur-manager.

Communicate and Market the Value Proposition

A difficult challenge for the entrepreneur-manager is to communicate the value proposition of his venture to key stakeholders. At Dow Chemical, for example, Ian Telford was worried that the company's epoxy leadership team (ELT) would reject his e-channel idea. Telford had tested the prototype of the site and put together a good business plan. He was concerned, however, because the vote to fund his exploratory study had been contentious, and he believed there were vested interests on the ELT who opposed his project. He wanted to do something dramatic to push home the importance of his venture.

Two weeks before a critical review meeting for his project, Telford started a rumor via e-mail claiming that a major competitive announcement was imminent. The rumor had a leading chemical distributor, two major chemical competitors, and an Internet company coming together to form a new Web-based joint venture. E-mails started flying, with mounting suspense over the impending announcement that weekend. Telford volunteered to have the show taped and flown in from the United Kingdom. He had already arranged to have a spoof broadcast videotaped using his friends as stand-ins for a news anchor, a financial analyst, the CEO of the new joint venture, and even an actual customer!

Sensing that he might be crossing the line, Telford showed the video to his boss, Philippe Raynaud de Fitte, and asked for his advice. The boss agreed to show the video but with some precautions, briefing members of the ELT that what they were about to watch was a spoof. Recalling that viewing, the then-chairman of the ELT noted, "Yes, the videotape annoyed me. There was no need for these antics. But it did serve as a wake-up call. The majority of the ELT became positive toward Telford's venture."

What Telford had managed to do visually was to alert internal stakeholders that the real competition was *outside* the firm and his venture was aimed at building a new competence, an e-channel, for Dow Chemical.

Some members of the ELT saw both the e-mail rumor chain and fake video as going a bit too far. It is the job of the project's sponsor to ensure that entrepreneur-managers' creative approaches to marketing their ideas do not violate the core values of the firm. Telford was coached on these transgressions. But, there was also an appreciation that giving the entrepreneur-manager some leeway on rules was essential to sustaining his energy and passion.

We mention the Telford example not to advocate such a radical approach to communicating the value proposition of a renewal project but instead to highlight that renewal ventures do attract internal resistance within the firm. Some will worry about the risks involved, others will be concerned by what the project means for their own performance, and yet others will worry about the size of the potential prize. Entrepreneur-managers must not only deal with these substantive concerns but also with the underlying emotional issues. Marketing a renewal project is not just a matter of formal presentations; it is also about informal lobbying and influencing key stakeholders.

Manage Stakeholders, Gain Support, and Mobilize Resources

Selling a build/leverage/transform project to key internal stakeholders is difficult. Even though we would expect the business and functional heads whose units are affected to take an enterprisewide view, parochial considerations do exist. The entrepreneur-manager must have the ability to deal with these competing interests.

For example, Ian Telford faced a lot of internal opposition to his e-channel idea in Dow Chemical. Product managers and country heads did not like the price transparency that the e-channel would bring. This had the potential to hurt the profitability of their units. Telford came up with a compromise idea, limiting the products and terms that would be offered on the e-channel and ensuring that the price offered was never lower than that available to the firm's best customers.

All the entrepreneur-managers we know are good at listening to their internal stakeholders, and they are flexible, but this does not mean they are easily swayed from their mission. In describing Telford's approach to these challenges, a manager who worked closely with him from the beginning of the e-epoxy.com project had this to say:

> *Ian has rich experience of the industry and deep marketing insights. He has exceptional ability to understand stakeholders and dance around minefields of vested interests. His strength is his breadth of grasp, but this is not superficial. He talks to all stakeholders, fully understands their concerns. However, this does not mean that he seeks okay from every one of them.*

Besides getting the buy-in from stakeholders on the strategy that the entrepreneur-manager wants to pursue, he also needs their support for necessary resources. We noted earlier how entrepreneur-managers seldom have all the resources they need to deliver on their goals. They need to tap into the knowledge and skills, available throughout the organization. For example, a big challenge for Telford was to get resources from the company's corporate information systems (IS) department.

The IS department was legitimately concerned that the exceptions that Telford's project would need made connectivity with other systems an issue. Also, his system would not be easily scalable, should the project become a success. Tracy Teich, IS director for the Thermoset business, recalled how Telford won them over:

> *The strength of the e-epoxy.com venture was that Telford had a well-articulated position. He had a credible story, and he told it well. Telford was also a model customer. He respected all the IS rules. He took great care in preparing the initial specifications and there were no major revisions as the project progressed. He met all the IS requirements, on time, every time. Some of the best*

IS architects volunteered for the project. Telford recognized their work and praised their efforts. When he received his first order, he took the trouble to call the IS team. This gave them instant ownership of the project.

Assemble and Motivate a Team of Experts

The entrepreneur-manager has to be a skilled manager of human talent, even more so than his peers in operations. This is because he does not have any special carrots to offer his team in exchange for the risk that they must take in working for him. The risks in joining a renewal project are twofold. First is that if the project fails, it can have negative career consequences. A more immediate concern is that salary increases and bonuses may also be at risk. Project teams assigned to renewal strategies tend to be small and concentrated on talent. However, most corporate reward systems insist on a forced ranking of employee performance. In a small, high-performing team, it will cause several talented individuals to be rated as par or even subpar. This is the risk that an employee takes in joining a renewal project.

Consider the challenge for Ganev when he launched the CTS project in Ericsson. He sought to hire some of his erstwhile colleagues in the Components Division of Ericsson Mobile for his project. Despite the risks in the CTS venture, five of them volunteered to work for Ganev. The excitement that Ganev was able to communicate for his project was one reason.

The other was Ganev had a reputation for providing a fun work environment and personally caring for his team members. He did not place that much faith in formal competence. It was more important for him that the members of his team be enthusiastic about their work and find their jobs both interesting and fun. Commenting on Ganev's people management skills, a senior human resources executive at Ericsson had this to say:

> *Most people Ganev employs stay in his organization for quite a long time and are very loyal and enthusiastic to the organization they have created. Ganev shows a genuine interest and devotion to his employees. This also includes their social and private lives.*

We encountered a similar story at HP. When Nick Earle launched the e-services initiative, the word got out that this could be fun. He had no problem putting together a team of "rebels," 12 employees who were "really frustrated with HP" and 5 outsiders. They started with two questions: *What is HP's Internet strategy? What should it be?* In a conference room next to his office, Earle set up the War Room. The door was locked (a novelty in HP's open-cubicle environment) and the window was blacked out. Many HP colleagues wondered what was going on in that room. What they did not know was that top researchers were pasting the walls with flipchart paper, trying to understand the technology requirements of the future. The sheer excitement of the task was the real motivation for the team.

Besides providing an island of fun and excitement, entrepreneur-managers also have to manage the career risks of their subordinates. When asked what would have happened if the e-epoxy venture had failed at Dow Chemical, Telford replied:

> *I think my career would have taken a hit. But I was not worried about that. I was more concerned with the experience to be gained and the future of my team members. Even though they volunteered to take on this risky assignment, I tried to develop "escape routes" for all of them. Given the high visibility that the venture had, I made sure that team members were placed in positions where senior executives would notice them if the worst came to the worst.*

Personal Traits

The four personal traits that we have noticed in successful entrepreneur-managers are a propensity to take risks, a passion and inner fire, an action orientation, and self-confidence.

Propensity to Take Risks

Entrepreneur-managers usually display an appetite for risk both in their personal and professional lives.

Personal Risks

Peter Francis is the chairman, president, and CEO of J.M. Huber Corporation, a diversified, multinational supplier of engineered materials, natural resources, and technology-based services. It is a fast-growing privately held company that celebrates entrepreneurship. Francis himself was an entrepreneur-manager before rising to head the company.

When Francis hires new managers, he looks for evidence of risk taking in the person's background—influenced perhaps by his own personal history. He and his wife had circumnavigated the world by sailboat, visiting 38 countries, covering 55,000 miles, and spending 558 days at sea. After that sea adventure, Francis went on to receive an MBA at Stanford and eventually settled into a very successful corporate career.

Francis is partial to applicants who have backgrounds that show evidence of personal risk taking, such as adventure, working for voluntary organizations in difficult conditions, running a small business, or any such experience. He would be the first to admit that he does not have a proven formula, but he would submit that a prior record of some risk taking in one's personal life is perhaps a good predictor of an appetite for risk taking in a corporate context.

Indeed, we found such a streak in some of the entrepreneur-managers we met. Ian Telford at Dow Chemical, for example, has a passion for adventurous sports such as ice climbing, off-piste skiing, and karate. Tsviatko Ganev, who worked for Ericsson in Sweden, was a refugee from communist Bulgaria and an outspoken critic of the then regime. But good ice climbers avoid accidents, and smart political critics don't get shot. We are talking about prudent risk taking here.

Professional Risks

Apart from taking prudent risks in their personal lives, entrepreneur-managers also take risks professionally. But here again, these are more prudent than the ones that external entrepreneurs take, like betting their personal assets—bank balance, home, boat, car—to pursue a dream.

But unlike many of their peer managers in the firm, entrepreneur-managers are much more likely to take career risks in the pursuit of projects that they are passionate about. As Rupert Gasser, a former senior vice president at Nestlé, notes:

> *The real barrier to innovation is perceived risk. People ask themselves, "Why should I engage in a process with an uncertain outcome?" People reject risk taking because they feel it can endanger their current status, their jobs.*

As a consequence of their risk-taking behaviors, entrepreneur-managers might not rise as fast as their peer group through the corporate hierarchy. Unfortunately, large companies tend to promote managers who have an uninterrupted record of success.

Implementing renewal strategies involves risk, with its attendant failures. It is hard to have uninterrupted success as an entrepreneur-manager.

Passion and Inner Fire

Entrepreneur-managers are passionate people. They will only sign on to projects that they care about; and after they commit, they invest themselves fully and emotionally in the project's goals. Describing this quality in Lang, the project manager for Nespresso, his superior Rupert Gasser remarked:

> *Lang was ambitious and strong-headed. He wanted to do something outstanding. Lang had personality; he was a force. There were not many people in the company who believed in Nespresso, but Lang did. He was totally convinced of the opportunity.*

Entrepreneur-managers own their projects and may appear obstinate, but it comes out of an inner conviction. At Ericsson, Ganev was described by his superior as follows:

> *Ganev is emotional and can be very stubborn. He is emotional because he throws himself entirely into his job and in serving our clients, and he's stubborn when he is sure the customer is being mistreated. So why don't we call it conviction instead of being stubborn?*

This inner fire is not unique to entrepreneur-managers. We have also seen it among other managers, when driving a quality- or process-improvement initiative, pruning or extending the company's product line, or even leading a tough restructuring effort. What distinguishes the two, however, is where this energy and inner fire are directed. In the case of the entrepreneur-manager, it is always directed outward toward leveraging a new opportunity or building a *new* capability, and not on optimizing what the firm already has. Entrepreneur-managers delight in doing *new* things. This is the side to their personality that most resembles an external entrepreneur.

On the flip side, when a project loses its novelty, the entrepreneur-manager's passion for it also drops. Telford at Dow Chemical described it as being as anticlimactic as "taking the final exam." The hard work is done. Instead of coasting on the fruits of that labor, the entrepreneur-manager wants the next challenge. When e-epoxy.com achieved breakeven and the new platform was established, Telford wanted to move on to the next challenge. The same was the case for Ganev at Ericsson and Lang at Nespresso.

This passionate commitment of the entrepreneur-manager to a renewal project brings a lot of energy to it and is vital for its success. When the passion ebbs, however, the energy can, too. Finding the next challenge and moving the entrepreneur-manager on to it at the right time is a major role of the project's sponsor.

An Action Orientation

Entrepreneur-managers are action oriented. They are not big on planning, but they will do what it takes to get funded. Executing the venture is more important to entrepreneur-managers than researching or talking about it. In fact, it is in the execution of a project that they learn how to shape it. An R&D vice president at Ericsson realized this simple truth and was skillful in inviting Ganev to "research" difficult issues for the company on four different occasions. Ganev responded every single time with a successful project. Each of these ventures lasted about five years.

The prime motivation for the entrepreneur-manager is to deliver results. Like Ganev at Ericsson, Telford at Dow Chemical got higher marks for execution than for planning. As one of his peers said:

> *Somebody with a better business idea probably would not have been able to bring such a diverse group of people together and to drive the idea through the required approvals of the business team. More than his idea, Telford deserves credit for his execution skills.*

The bragging rights for Telford were not that he had pursued an innovative idea but that he had delivered the project on time and under budget. Entrepreneur-managers like to be judged by their actions, not their words.

When confronted with obstacles, entrepreneur-managers are also not averse to challenging the bureaucratic ways of large corporations. In that respect, they differ from many operating managers, who are far more compliant.

Consider the case of Ganev at Ericsson. He was up against the company's rules that restricted overtime pay. However, he had to engage his team in overtime work to meet the tight deadlines for his project. Ganev found a loophole in the system that allowed him to bypass this rule. He moved his project to a subsidiary company and arranged to get his employees "special financial compensation," not overtime pay.

But entrepreneur-managers, like Ganev, know which rules to bend. Although they can ask for—and often receive—forgiveness for bypassing operating procedures that hinder speedy implementation, they are careful not to violate procedures that embody the core values of the firm.

Self-Confidence

Entrepreneurial projects are risky, and they can fail. It is important that the entrepreneur-manager learns from his or her mistakes and either makes mid-course corrections or pulls the plug. Talking about his experiences on the CTS project at Ericsson, one of Ganev's collaborators noted:

> *When Ganev has a goal or a plan, he pushes it until he gets a result or he finds that he cannot reach his goal. When he realizes he can't reach his goal, he changes the plan, and the action.*

We believe there is an important personal trait that helps entrepreneur-managers to accept their mistakes. It is their immense self-confidence in their own abilities. When a project fails, they do not take it personally. They genuinely feel that no one else could have managed it better.

Professional Experience

We believe that professional experience is another important element in the profile of an entrepreneur-manager. There are two aspects to this experience: track record and length and quality of tenure.

Established Track Record

It is said that successful venture capitalists bet on the jockey more so than on the horse or the race—that is, on the track record of the venture manager more so than on the venture itself or the industry that it is in. This is equally true when implementing renewal strategies. The track record of the entrepreneur-manager matters a lot. It buys him freedom to operate and the trust of his senior managers.

Consider the LC1 project, for example. Gallagher realized that the French launch was a disappointment. Instead of hiding this, he increased commitment levels and sought the help of his superiors to relaunch the product in Germany. Gallagher could do that because he had earned their trust through a proven prior performance record. Even if the LC1 venture was in trouble, given his successful track record, he knew that he himself would not be seen as a failure.

Long Tenure

Entrepreneur-managers seldom have all the resources they need to deliver on their goals, so they have to borrow them from elsewhere in the organization. It takes time to know who the best sources are for these resources. But, the lending unit might have no incentive to cooperate; it usually has its own priorities. To borrow, it helps if the borrower was a lender previously or is a prospective lender in the future. Establishing this kind of reciprocity can take time. It is unlikely, therefore, that successful entrepreneur-managers will have spent less than five years in their companies. It takes at least that long to establish trust and a network of support within the firm.

Four of the entrepreneur-managers we studied were successful mid-level managers with long track records in their companies. They also had the opportunity to move through multiple functions/countries/businesses. They had a wide range of contacts inside the firm and had established strong internal networks, both through their own competencies that made others ask them for help and through a track record of giving and not just taking. Gallagher, for example, was highly networked in

Nestlé's R&D and marketing organizations. This allowed him to expedite the product launch in France and move quickly to Germany when the French initiative was a failure. Andrea Pfeifer, a lead scientist at the Nestlé Research Center, was an important partner, as were market experts in France, Germany, and at the corporate headquarters. Gallagher's skill was in "borrowing with pride" from all parts of Nestlé.

Exception to the Rule

As noted previously, we do not believe that successful entrepreneur-managers can be hired from the outside. They have to be developed inside the firm. Although personal traits help, it takes experience to develop the skills, business knowledge, and organizational network that is needed for success. However, one exception applies to this rule: a transformation strategy. Unlike the build or leverage initiatives that are anchored in either the firm's existing markets or distinctive competencies, a transform initiative seeks to explore an opportunity that is new on both dimensions.

Consider the Nespresso project. A new manager, Yannick Lang, was hired from outside Nestle to lead the separate, 100 percent Nestlé-owned company, Nespresso, which was established specifically to develop the Nespresso system. Camille Pagano, at the time a senior executive vice president in charge of several worldwide strategic product divisions and business units, commented on this move:

> We needed to find somebody who wouldn't react like a Nestlé manager. People in our organization are good, but at the time, everyone was asking, "How could we sell this thing in supermarkets?" Nestlé doesn't bring people in from the outside as a common practice, but we needed someone who understood what it meant to sell a premium system—something between Louis

Vuitton fashion accessories and Maggi bouillon. This needs a special mentality. What really convinced me was Lang's background, coming from Philip Morris where going to the clothing business was also a stab in the dark; it was not the usual thing to do.

Indeed, external hires might be needed from time to time, especially to execute a transformation strategy. The new mindset required may just not be available inside the firm. However, unless the new venture is planned to be standalone—isolated from the core—it will need resources and expertise from other parts of the firm. Lacking a network within the firm, the external hire will need, at least initially, the help of senior managers to access the required internal resources. In the case of Nespresso, senior executives like Pagano at Nestlé provided this help to Lang.

Summary

Managing a leverage, build, or transform strategy needs a special type of manager—an entrepreneur-manager.

These entrepreneur managers are in part corporate entrepreneurs. They are outward-focused, cognizant of changes in their business environment and the new opportunities that these may bring. They are willing to experiment with new business models and to explore new capabilities. However, they are also operating managers interested in scaling up an entrepreneurial idea and in delivering results.

Entrepreneur-managers are especially skilled at discovering a valuable business proposition for their ventures, communicating and marketing this to all stakeholders within the firm, mobilizing the necessary resources even when they have no authority over these, assembling and motivating a team of experts, and most important, delivering results. These skills can be learned. In fact, they are often the focus of leadership-development programs that we have run in many companies. But what is typically missing is the chance to apply these skills in a high-risk and resource-scarce business environment, like those associated with renewal strategies of leverage, build, and transform. These skills can be honed only through practice, through trial and error, under the watchful eye of a good coach.

Entrepreneur-managers have a few special personality traits. They are not risk averse and will take risks with their careers. They are action oriented and have the energy and inner fire to make their venture a success. Although they might bend a few rules in the process, they always stay true to the corporate vision and values. Entrepreneur-managers are also supremely self-confident. These traits allow them to take more risks, persist despite failures, and learn from their mistakes.

Entrepreneur-managers are typically not newcomers to the organization. Their long tenure helps with networking inside the firm. They also have an established track record of performing well. That buys them the freedom to operate outside the usual confines of the organization and enjoy the trust needed to take risks on behalf of the firm. Assigning a short-tenure manager to a high-risk renewal strategy abridges the support network that is available to it. This arrangement is likely to fail.

CHAPTER 6

Sponsoring Renewal

"True entrepreneur-managers are able to identify new opportunities and to empower their teams even in situations of great uncertainty. But in order to be successful, they need a sponsor, who sets tough, stretching goals, and demands results; but is also accessible and able to coach when necessary, and above all can tolerate failure'."

—Matti Alahuhta, CEO, Kone

As you saw in the preceding chapter, entrepreneur-managers are the engines that drive continuous renewal. Behind every successful entrepreneur-manager, however, there is an effective sponsor. Sponsors are senior executives, usually heads of business divisions or regions such as in the renewal initiatives at Dow, HP, and Nestlé that we discussed in the preceding chapter; or heads of functions such as R&D or new business development, as in the case of the Ericsson example. Occasionally, the CEO himself may be the sponsor, as in the case of Best Buy—a company we discussed at length in Chapter 3, "Continuous Renewal."

The effective sponsors we know do not have any particular personality profile. They come from a variety of backgrounds. Only a few of them have been entrepreneur-managers before. If anything, having been a successful entrepreneur-manager can handicap a sponsor. Such a sponsor would have to hold back the temptation to second-guess the entrepreneur-manager on every move. Sponsorship differs from entrepreneurship.

Good sponsors are well-respected senior executives with an excellent track record of delivering results. They need the accumulated credibility to perform their jobs well. Sponsors are also distinguished by the skills that they display in performing five critical roles: (1) defining the scope of a renewal project, (2) finding the entrepreneur-manager to run it, (3) locating a suitable organizational home for the project, (4) tailoring the firm's control and incentives systems to help with its implementation, and (5) coaching and supporting the entrepreneur-manager. We discuss each of these roles in this chapter.

In some companies, such as Dow Chemical, DuPont, and Shell, there are mentors in addition to sponsors. Whereas sponsors guide the entrepreneur-manager on business issues, the mentor is primarily concerned with the personal development of the entrepreneur-manager. We believe that this can be a useful complement to what the sponsor does. However, it is also the responsibility of the sponsor to develop the entrepreneur-manager as an individual, and not just support the renewal project that he manages.

Defining the Scope of a Renewal Project

Although entrepreneur-managers must be given the freedom to be creative, it is equally important to ensure that this creativity is properly channeled. Unlike an external entrepreneur, the entrepreneur-manager cannot direct his passion and energy to the goals he chooses. These have to be channeled to serve a corporate purpose. Making that happen is the primary responsibility of the sponsor. A good sponsor understands the corporate purpose and strategy of the firm and translates these into a renewal agenda for the businesses that he manages.

With the help of his executive team, the sponsor deliberates on questions such as these: How can profitability and growth be sustained? What are the emerging opportunities and threats? What are the critical leverage, build, and transform initiatives that should be considered? What resources should be earmarked for these? Based on these discussions, he defines a broad template for the renewal projects that he will support.

This template is not a plan, but more of a guide to determine areas where creative new ideas are needed. The ideas that emerge from the organization might not neatly converge with these needs. As we discuss later in this section, renewal strategies are finally shaped through interactions and iterations in the planning process.

Recall the e-epoxy.com venture at Dow Chemical from the preceding chapter. It was Ian Telford's divisional president, Henri Vermaak, together with his epoxy leadership team, who had put together a strategy template for improving the growth and profitability of the epoxy business. They had identified three customer segments: key accounts that would be serviced directly by the company's sales force, mid-size accounts that would be serviced by the firm's dealers, and a third segment consisting of smaller and infrequent customers that the company found hard to serve profitably. This was a potential opportunity for the company, provided it could develop a new low-cost distribution channel for accessing these customers.

Ian Telford, the entrepreneur-manager, had just returned from a company-sponsored training program on the potential uses of the Internet, an emerging technology at that time. He saw a connection between the needs of the company and the new tool that he had been trained on. He proposed the e-epoxy.com project to serve this unserved segment. His excitement was around applying the Internet, a novelty at that time, to pioneer a new sales channel for Dow Chemical.

As we suggested in Chapter 1, "The Performance Dilemmas," the firm needs to steer the middle path between the two extremes of everything planned and prescribed by senior executives to everything emergent and improvised by the entrepreneur-manager. Like in the e-epoxy.com project, shaping a renewal strategy is in part top down—a karaoke orchestra where the music is preset. In part, however, it is also like a jazz concert, allowing creative new initiatives to emerge—the music is more

extemporary. Neither is sufficient; what is needed is a blend—
karaoke jazz.

Designing such a blended context is not easy, but that is the
need. Our own research has shown how this balance can be
shaped by managing the interactions and iterations in the firm's
planning process.

Interactions and Iterations in Planning

Interactions in the planning process refer to the communication
between the sponsor and the entrepreneur-manager in shaping the
firm's renewal strategies. The greater the interaction, the richer the
alternatives that are considered, and the better the alignment with
the corporate vision. Highlighting the importance of high
interaction, Bob Wood, a former group president of the
Thermoset business at Dow Chemical, had this to say:

> *It is the senior executive who should connect a venture proposal to
> a big strategic opportunity for the company. It is key to spend a
> lot of time in the front end of the venture, to sit down and discuss
> the data, the idea, suggest what the timing for the investment
> should be, what group of people should be involved in the project,
> ask a number of questions, check the enthusiasm of the team,
> ensure that they are agile, and make sure that they are getting
> data from actions and not necessarily waiting for all the final
> details to make a decision and then to act. We have to learn to
> make decisions in that zone of discomfort.*

According to Wood, the interaction was important not only to
communicate the renewal agenda of the sponsor and learn about
the ideas that the entrepreneur-manager had for supporting it but
also to look him in the eye and see whether there was "fire in his
belly." Was he the right person to head the renewal project? If

there was already a team in place, did it have the right members? Who else should be on the team? Where should the project be housed? The time that the sponsor spends up front on a renewal project is critical to its success. The more risky the project, the greater the need for repeated and rich interactions between the sponsor and entrepreneur-manager.

Another design consideration is the degree of iteration in the planning process. There are typically three distinct phases in a strategic planning process: agenda setting, strategic programming, and budgeting. The first of these phases refers to the sharing and translation of the firm's vision into individual goals, whether for running operations or managing renewal projects. In the strategic programming phase, the attempt is to explore alternative means of achieving these goals and to put together a multiyear program of action. In the budgeting phase, yearly resource commitments are made to implement part of this approved program.

When the three phases are followed in a rigid sequential fashion, goals are frozen before strategic programs are developed, and programs are fixed before budgets are decided. There is no iteration in the planning process. By contrast, when each phase is seen more as a guide for the next without rigidly constraining it, the planning process is more iterative. In an *iterative* process, goals, programs, and budgets influence each other, and they can all change during the planning exercise.

All renewal strategies involve a trial-and-error learning process. The original strategy, or even the project's goals, may have to be modified through this learning; and on occasion, the project might have to be abandoned altogether. The greater the risk in a renewal strategy, the greater the need for frequent iterations.

Although the case for customizing the interactions and iterations in the planning process to suit the renewal strategy may be intuitively appealing, often there are countervailing pressures to have a one-size-fits-all planning system. There are merits to this approach, too. These include simplicity and efficiency. The forms, procedures, and models used can be standardized. A standard system makes it easy to compare rival investments and consolidate financial projections. It is also cheaper to support.

By focusing on interactions between managers and iterations between phases of the planning system, we have shifted the onus for customizing the planning process to senior managers and how they choose to engage with the system rather than tinker with the mechanics of the system. The mechanics, such as the forms and formats used, and the analytical models and expert support that is provided can be standard. However, the process itself can be tailored depending on how senior managers choose to engage with it.

We distinguish between two types of engagement (see Table 6.1). In an integrative process, the sponsor sets stretch goals in a top-down fashion and insists on a strict sequencing of the subsequent strategic programming and budgeting phases with very little iteration between them. Five-year financial projections in the program are linked tightly to the corresponding yearly budgets with little leeway for change. Variance from budget is interpreted strictly to mean failed implementation; it is not used to reshape the underlying strategic program or reset the associated goals. In fact, the sponsor's time is heavily geared toward the budgeting phase. Entrepreneur-managers will see such a planning process as nothing more than a giant budgeting exercise. Such an integrative planning process is not conducive to any of the renewal strategies.

In an adaptive process, by contrast, goals are negotiated with the entrepreneur-manager through rich interaction. Sponsors participate frequently when alternative strategies are mapped and the strategic program is defined. Also, because budgets, programs, and goals are reviewed frequently and revised iteratively, sponsors may choose to spend less of their time on the budgeting phase.

Table 6.1

Tailoring the Planning Process

Process ~~(Sponsor Roles)~~	Integrative	Adaptive
Goal setting	Top down	Participative
Time spending pattern	Back end (mostly on budgeting)	Front end (mostly on strategic programming)
Linking programs and budgets	Very tight and strict sequencing	Relatively loose and highly iterative

All renewal strategies need some elements of an adaptive process. The intensity of the interactions and iterations grows with the underlying risk in each renewal strategy—ranging from low in the case of a protect and extend strategy, moderate for a leverage or build strategy, to high in the case of a transform strategy. There are no precise metrics to define this scale. Applying it is a matter of judgment. Recognizing that the interactions and iterations in the planning process would have to be different, depending on the renewal strategy that is being sponsored, is more important.

Consider the launching of Nespresso at Nestlé. Its planning required frequent interactions between the company's corporate leaders (including the CEO and two senior executive sponsors), its corporate research and commercial staff, the Nespresso project manager Yannick Lang, and his team of engineers and marketers. The project also needed frequent iterations. The original goal of selling Nespresso to offices was shelved in favor of going to the restaurant market, before being shelved yet again to go after residential consumers. The idea of selling capsules direct via mail order through the Nespresso Club was also an emergent idea and not part of the initial plan.

Moving away from the core requires experimentation, more interactions, and iterations in planning. The sponsor must be able to make these time commitments.

Staffing the Renewal Project

Sponsors face two distinct challenges in staffing a renewal project: (1) spotting budding entrepreneur-managers and assigning them to the right project, and (2) managing the careers of established entrepreneur-managers.

Budding Entrepreneur-Managers

The profile of an entrepreneur-manager that we provided in the preceding chapter is a good starting point for the search. We had described four personal traits: propensity to take risks, passion and inner fire, action orientation, and self-confidence; and four skills: seeing the big picture, communicating the business value of the project, managing stakeholders and mobilizing resources, and assembling and motivating a team of experts.

As we emphasized in that chapter, however, budding entrepreneur-managers are typically not newcomers to the firm. They have a track record. Their personnel records should provide information on their personal traits, skills, and experience. However, in our experience, entrepreneur-managers are not spotted through a systematic screening of their personnel records.

Budding entrepreneur-managers announce themselves. Remember, they are self-confident and are always looking for new experiences. Senior managers who have a reputation for being good sponsors attract their fair share of inquiries and proposals from budding entrepreneur-managers. Not all these aspirants will have the desired traits, especially risk taking. They have to be screened out. Others may lack the experience or not be very proficient in the skills required. If the sponsor believes that these individuals can be developed into effective entrepreneur-managers, however, they should be given a chance—starting with lower-risk renewal projects. How else would they acquire the needed experience?

An important role that senior managers play in supporting renewal is to spot budding entrepreneur-managers and help in their development.

Established Entrepreneur-Managers

Established entrepreneur-managers enjoy a great deal of respect within the firm for the successes that they have achieved. Their somewhat irreverent style also attracts a cult-like following among subordinate employees (as well as a tinge of annoyance from higher ups and peers). One senior executive refers to this special band of managers as "James Bonds." Sponsors know who they are and what idiosyncrasies they bring to the job.

Like the famous spy hero, entrepreneur-managers take risks, can mobilize the resources that they need, and ignore the bureaucratic rules of the firm. But, they are always loyal to the assigned mission and deliver results most of the time. The executive goes on to observe: "Grateful as I am for these James Bonds, I am also glad that we have only a few of them. Imagine a company where everyone has a license to kill!" Entrepreneur-managers need special care.

Finding the right project for an established entrepreneur-manager is not easy. It is important to note here that the entrepreneur-manager does not have to be an expert on the technical or commercial aspects of a renewal project. There are others on his team who will play that role. Recall the renewal projects from the preceding chapter. Telford was not an expert on the Internet and yet he was assigned the e-epoxy.com project. Lang was not the expert on the Nespresso system and yet he ran that project quite successfully. More than subject matter expertise, what the sponsor should look for is whether the project will satisfy the learning and ego needs of the entrepreneur-manager.

The project offered must present new learning opportunities. It has to resonate with the inner fire of the entrepreneur-manager. Also, the more experienced the entrepreneur-manager, the more important the assigned project has to be to the firm. Being challenged by a high-visibility project is a huge motivator for the entrepreneur-manager. In the Ericsson example from the preceding chapter, the sponsor Jan Uddenfeldt—the then-head of R&D, was very skilled at finding challenging projects for Tsviatko Ganev, the entrepreneur-manager. The CTS project, aimed at finding a cheaper and more flexible cellular transmission system, was just one in a sequence of four challenges over two decades.

If a sponsor does not have the next big project for the entrepreneur-manager, it is equally important that he is released for another opportunity elsewhere in the firm. Lobbying for and finding that opportunity is the responsibility of the sponsor.

Also, not all entrepreneur-managers may aspire to manage progressively more difficult and riskier projects. Some entrepreneur-managers may prefer to go back to the operating organization. Gallagher and Lang at Nestlé moved on to manage other more traditional businesses within the company before leaving to explore opportunities outside. Telford went on to an operating role and has done well within Dow Chemical. Managing these career transitions is also part of the sponsor's responsibility. Entrepreneur-managers are not the obvious pick for senior-line positions, even though it would do a world of good to have senior managers in the company with firsthand experience of running renewal projects. The sponsor might have to push for this.

Locating a Proper Organizational Home

Locating the renewal project in the right home is another challenge for the sponsor. Most large companies are organized in what is called a *transnational matrix*, with businesses, geographies, and functions as the three dimensions of this matrix. In theory, each dimension should work in perfect harmony with the other— with the business dimension focused on global efficiency, the geography dimension on local responsiveness, and the functional dimension on enterprisewide sharing and learning. Often, however, the efficiency consideration trumps the others. As Hans Ulrich Maerki, chairman of IBM Europe, Middle East, and Africa, remarked candidly:

> The "perfect" matrix is often tightly interlocked. There is no breathing space to do any innovation. We have launched a separate European Business Opportunity (EBO) initiative. But an EBO that is separated from the core is difficult, and transplanting any of the results back to the core is hard.

Indeed, surveys by leading management consulting firms such as the Boston Consulting Group and McKinsey show that the structure commonly used in today's corporations is no more than a thinly disguised classic command-and-control structure. For reasons of simplicity and sharper accountability, corporate leaders prefer to focus on a single dimension of the organizational matrix, often favoring global efficiency to the exclusion of growth and innovation. Innovation is pursued through separate initiatives (for example, the EBO at IBM). But as Maerki points out, the organizational challenge is to give these initiatives enough autonomy to thrive but without severing their connectedness to the core.

We have seen three types of homes for renewal projects: standalone subsidiaries, new venture organizations, and corporate projects; these provide varying balance between autonomy and connectedness.

Standalone Subsidiaries

Standalone subsidiaries are established outside the mainstream businesses, primarily to give the renewal initiatives autonomy. Two examples are the Nespresso subsidiary at Nestlé, a case that you have seen before, and the Playstation subsidiary at Sony. Their isolation ensured that the new initiatives did not get bogged down in the bureaucracy of the larger structure and had more freedom to emphasize their uniqueness. The standalone subsidiaries typically report directly to a senior sponsor and are funded directly from a corporate budget.

This structural arrangement can be very helpful to execute a transform strategy. Indeed, as you saw earlier, Nespresso was successful in building a new business model for Nestlé, entering an upscale consumer segment with a premium product and through a direct channel. Without this structure, the Nespresso idea might have languished within the Nescafé division of Nestlé. Similarly, Playstation allowed Sony to get into entertainment software, away from the hardware focus of its core Electronics Products Group. In these and other cases, the arguments in favor of a standalone subsidiary are clear. It provides focus, minimizes interference, attracts dedicated funding, and concentrates accountability. Senior managers can readily monitor the progress of a renewal initiative that is housed independently, rather than buried within the matrix structure of the firm.

However, the problem with such strict partitioning is that it can create unintended organizational boundaries and limit the flow of information and ideas to and from the subsidiary. The standalone subsidiary may not fully benefit from the many distinctive competencies and market access that the core businesses can provide. New businesses segregated from the core businesses usually lack close contact with key customers, technology providers, and competitors, contacts that often generate promising new opportunities. In turn, it is difficult at a later date to integrate the ideas that come out of this subsidiary back into the core, either by leveraging their potential with the resources in the core or renewing the core with the new competencies that may have been acquired. Making these connections is the burden of the sponsor. The subsidiary manager might not have much of an incentive to connect with the core.

Consider the Nespresso example again. It was consciously positioned when launched to serve the high-end consumer. In the recent past, there has been growing competition at the low end. For example, Senseo[1] is a low-end espresso coffee system sold by Sara Lee's Douwe Egbert's division in partnership with Philips. Its machines are less complicated than Nespresso's; the coffee comes in pods, not hermetically sealed individual capsules as it does with Nespresso. Senseo may not produce as strong a cup of espresso as the Nespresso system, but it has found a niche. First introduced in the Netherlands in 2001, Senseo is sold today on four continents. As of 2006, 12 million Senseo machines had been sold worldwide, and it was expected to generate sales of $500 million by fiscal 2007. Clearly, there was a market opportunity for Nestlé at the low end.

In parallel, Nestlé's Nescafé division has introduced its own coffee systems—the Nescafé Dolce Gusto, to deliver four different specialty coffees at the "touch of your fingertip," being the latest. That machine uses coffee and milk pods like the Senseo machine and is closer to Senseo than Nespresso in terms of its positioning and strategy. With initial entry only into the United Kingdom, Swiss, and German markets, the Dolce Gusto machines have been a big success. Nescafé has sold more than six million of its machine systems. Clearly, there is an opportunity here for Nespresso and Nescafé to coordinate their strategies. Making that happen is the role of senior management.

When the primary agenda of the standalone subsidiary is transformational—seeking to build a new business that is very different from the core—its relative isolation may not be an issue. When greater connectivity is needed, however, like in the case of a leverage or build strategy, there has to be a more formal link with the core businesses of the firm. Nokia, the world leader in mobile telephony, illustrates one such arrangement.

New Venture Organizations

In 1998, Nokia established the Nokia Ventures Organization (NVO). NVO was tasked with developing and proving innovative ideas that had the potential to generate revenues between $500 million and $1 billion for the company within four to five years.

The purpose of NVO was to look at growth opportunities that were beyond the normal scope of Nokia's two core businesses of Net (Nokia Networks) and NMP (Nokia Mobile Phones).

The NVO relied on its own work and on the basic research conducted by the Nokia Research Center for new ideas. The NVO was primarily meant to "accelerate" these ideas; but to give it enough autonomy, its projects were funded and closely monitored by corporate HQ.

As Matti Alahuhta, a Nokia senior executive until 2004, recalled, the thrust of the NVO was to look for ideas not "far from the core" but adjacent to it. A large number of these ideas were around new technologies, applications, or features that could enhance Nokia's competitive advantage in its core businesses. Many were eventually integrated back into the core. The Nokia Ventures board, which had representatives from the NVO, the Nokia Research Center, and the core businesses, decided on which ideas to move to the NVO. The board also ensured that there was a high probability of bringing the resulting ventures back to the core. Although new ideas could, in theory, also be spun off or divested, this rarely happened.

The Nokia NVO is an interesting approach to providing autonomy to the renewal initiative while still retaining links to the core business. In Nokia's approach, the sponsor's role is critical for ensuring that the NVO is used to develop and implement a full range of renewal strategies, including leverage, build, and even an occasional transform project—and not just projects that protect and extend the core.

If build and leverage are the renewal strategies of interest, another approach used by Sharp, the Japanese consumer electronics giant, should be of interest.

Corporate Projects

At Sharp, instead of setting up a standalone subsidiary, its top management has established what it calls Urgent Projects. Other companies use a similar corporate project concept. At Shell, for example, they are called elephant projects—elephant to signify the huge growth opportunity that these projects must bring to the firm.

A corporate committee identifies unmet customer needs or the missing technology seeds in all of Sharp's businesses. A cross-business, cross-functional team is then assembled by corporate to address this challenge, under the leadership of a senior executive—the team's sponsor. It is a full-time team for the entire duration of the project. The team goals are either to "create new technology seeds to serve identified market needs" (build initiatives) or to "identify new market needs for available technology seeds" (leverage initiatives).

Corporate project teams typically have four distinct characteristics:

> **Full-time members**—This is an important requirement. Although it is easy to launch a project with part-time members, it is hard to maintain momentum if members' loyalties are divided. The short-term performance pressures on team members from their operating responsibilities are likely to trump the longer-term team agenda of exploring for either new "technology seeds or market needs."

> **Face-to-face (not virtual) teams**—This is particularly important for the core members of the team, when the build or leverage agenda is ambitious. Breakthrough ideas come at unscheduled moments of intensive brainstorming. This can only happen with face-to-face teams.

> **Diverse teams**—Teams have to be diverse in terms of the skills and experience represented, blending multiple functions, business, and seniority. Corporate management arranged the staffing of the Urgent Project teams at Sharp. Even though such teams may nominally be housed within a lead division, their staffing should not be restricted only to the talent that division can provide.
> **Corporate funding**—The funding for the corporate project team is provided by corporate. This ensures that the resources meant for growth initiatives are not diverted to the short-term operational needs of the lead division.

Renewal projects can also be sponsored by a business division (rather than the corporate office). The way to manage these is identical to the corporate project teams, except the funding comes from the division and not the corporate office.

Where to house the special project is another question for the sponsor. Ideally, it has to be in a division or business unit that is close to the new market opportunity or competencies that the project is seeking to access. There is tacit knowledge about these in the host unit that can best be accessed by locating the team within that unit. As a corporate project team member told us:

> *You can walk into anyone's office. You are treated as a member of the family. You do not have to sign a "visitor's" log or ask for formal permission before talking to folks who know the market or the competence that you are trying to develop.*

Consider the CTS project example at Ericsson, from the preceding chapter. Its sponsor Jan Uddenfeldt recognized early that where it was housed would be crucial to its success. He placed the project in a division that was strongly market focused (a competence that CTS needed to build). It was also as an unconsolidated subsidiary. That gave the project relatively more autonomy.

Unfortunately, the task of finding a proper divisional or business unit home for a renewal project is all too often left to the ingenuity of entrepreneur-managers. The wrong home for the project can stifle its renewal potential. The sponsor's role here is crucial. He has to ensure that the project is located in the right organizational home.

Tailoring the Context for Implementation

Detailing and implementing a renewal project is the responsibility of the entrepreneur-manager. The sponsor has an important role to play, too: setting a context that enforces the right discipline and providing the right rewards and recognition, as is appropriate to the risk profile of the project.

Discipline in Execution

Controlling entrepreneurship would appear to be an oxymoron. But all projects, regardless of how creative they are, must be controlled. There are two aspects that are salient here: what should be controlled and how.

Financial control systems must naturally be standardized, built around certain key measures that can be applied across the firm. The dilemma, however, is that standard measures can also be biased, often favoring short-term financial performance over longer-term growth. In one of the companies we researched, there was a heavy emphasis on improving EBITDA (earnings before interest, taxes, and dividends). This measure is excellent if the goal is to maximize utilization of the firm's asset base. The problem, however, is that in markets that already enjoy a relatively high EBITDA, new product introduction can only dilute EBITDA in the short run. New product introductions can get delayed or even abandoned as a result. Clearly, what to control should depend on the strategy being monitored.

It is useful here to distinguish the capital and expense budgets needed to maintain the momentum of a business from those required to implement strategic programs for future growth and profitability. We call the former the *momentum budget* and the latter the *renewal budget* (see Figure 6.1). Ideally, all entrepreneur-managers should have both budgets, but their relative mix will vary depending on the renewal strategy that they manage. A protect and extend strategy will typically require a smaller renewal budget than a transform strategy.

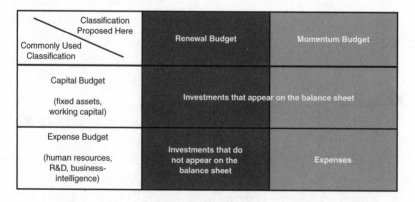

Figure 6.1
The twin budgets.

We have used the terms *momentum* and *renewal budgets* merely to describe an important idea.[2] None of the firms we researched uses these particular terms, but many practice the separation. Typically, there are line items in the operating budget that are meant for renewal initiatives. These should be monitored separately. Any savings here may merely signal that a renewal initiative has been delayed, not that new efficiencies have been gained.

Consider the case of Best Buy. Recognizing that customer-centricity was an experimental idea, Concept VII started as a trial in 32 of its stores; each of the laboratory stores at Best Buy incurred added expenses of around $300,000 a year. The major cost components were in employee training, the additional personnel required in each store, and increased inventory-carrying costs. An additional $200,000 to $300,000 per store was also required in one-time capital expenditure, mostly related to store remodeling, a new customer support center, and changes in signage. There was little incentive for managers of the trial stores to take on these additional capital expenditures and operating expenses. Although the anticipated growth in both sales and margins could provide offsetting benefits, these were in no way guaranteed. The top management of Best Buy treated the added operating and capital expenses in its trial stores as corporate costs—a de facto renewal budget.

On the question of how to control, the momentum and renewal budgets are qualitatively different. The output delivered against what was promised is a good measure of performance for the momentum budget. However, the renewal budget has a longer time horizon. The promised outputs might not be realizable within a single budget year. The entrepreneur-manager should not be unfairly punished for taking a long view. It may be more appropriate in this case to measure whether the promised effort in the renewal budget was expended and whether the corresponding milestones were actually reached. Also, failure to meet the promised milestones may not point only to performance shortcomings but in fact may suggest that the chosen strategy or even goals need to be revised. Renewal requires trial and error; in monitoring this effort, corporate leaders cannot ask for *error-free* execution.

Pulling the plug quickly when a project begins to stall is another key skill that senior managers must have. Although it is true that the more you work on something, the better the chance of a breakthrough, it is equally true that after you have worked on something for awhile, it is tough to give it up. That is the dilemma. The sponsor must avoid getting caught in a vicious cycle of escalating commitments to a failing experiment. A simple rule is to abandon a project when the experiment does not yield the positive results that were expected of it before either the money or time allocated to it runs out. Best Buy had to divest a chain of music stores that it had bought just a couple of years prior, when it recognized that its forays into shopping malls were a failed experiment. The divestment cost the company $400 million in write-offs, but it was better to take this hit quickly than invest further in a failed idea.

More generally, renewal strategies call for experimentation. Not all trials will succeed. Many may fail. Consider the case of Canon, the Japanese company with a long history of renewal.[3] Canon was founded in 1933 and focused predominantly on the production of world-class 35mm cameras. In 1962, when top management sensed that the camera business was maturing and not capable of fueling the company's growth, it created a new R&D division for the development of new products. Since then, that division has experimented with several business ideas. Figure 6.2 sketches Canon's evolution. The company is today a global leader in printers, copiers, and cameras. But along the way, it has had many failures and some successes. The company learned from each of its failures. It built new competencies that later proved useful for supporting other business experiments.

The company first leveraged its competencies in optics, mechanics, and miniaturization (based on its leading position in the 35mm camera business) to enter the market for 8mm cameras and mid-market cameras. Even though these forays were unsuccessful and quickly dropped, they built and strengthened competencies in microelectronics. Canon then leveraged these competencies to enter the calculator market, once again a flop. However, it hung on to its competencies and added to them new skills in the use of fine chemicals. This consolidated platform allowed Canon to enter and succeed in the photocopier market. The associated competencies that it built in microchip technologies allowed the company to attempt entry into the proprietary integrated circuits and large-scale computing businesses. Although these, again, were not successes, the company built new skills in optoelectronics, which have helped in its successful entry into the office-automation business.

There are important lessons in the Canon story for a sponsor. Renewal is risky, and failure should be expected for projects that seek to leverage, build, or transform (as in the Canon example). Far too often, a failed idea is closely associated with the manager executing it. Either the manager is fired unfairly, or in trying to protect that manager's reputation, a sponsor can make escalating commitments to a failed idea. The execution discipline suffers as a consequence.

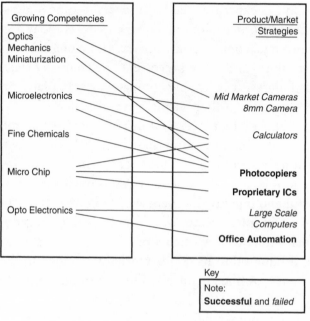

Figure 6.2
Trial-and-error learning at Canon.

The key role of the sponsor is to ensure that in case of project failures, and there will be plenty, there is an objective assessment of whether it was the idea or manager who failed. Sponsors should tolerate idea failures but not condone manager failures.

Rewards and Recognition

Over the years, incentive systems have been perfected, and sophisticated tools are available for determining performance bonuses and stock options. However, the push to make these objective and quantitative has made incentive systems better suited to maintaining the current momentum of a business and not help in its renewal. Build/leverage/transform initiatives, in particular, might not deliver top-line growth or bottom-line profits in the early years of investment. The quality of the effort expended by managers leading these initiatives may have to be judged more by the milestones they meet and a subjective assessment of the quality of their effort.

This does not mean entrepreneur-managers should be granted salary increases and bonuses based on these subjective assessments. They do not expect this. What they look for is recognition when they put out a quality effort, and a large bonus and even a promotion only when their projects succeed. It is even more important to entrepreneur-managers that their sponsors can distinguish between a failed idea and a failed effort. An idea failure should not be career limiting.

The entrepreneur-manager also seeks senior management attention. It is a key part of their motivation. Fernand Kaufmann, former corporate vice president for new business and strategic development at Dow Chemical, noted: "More than the hard stuff, the soft stuff—like the ability to interact more with senior management than their peers—seems to be a motivator. Visible public recognition is important."

Close interactions with the sponsor play a major role in reducing the alienation of the entrepreneur-manager to the firm. Even if the final decision goes against the entrepreneur-manager, if interactions with the sponsor are perceived to be of high quality, the entrepreneur-manager will remain committed to the firm and maintain his passion to drive other renewal initiatives.

And yet, entrepreneur-managers do not like to be seen as agents of senior management. This touch of irreverence is also part of the persona of an entrepreneur-manager. Sponsors have to be sensitive to this ambivalence, providing support and access while remaining detached from the everyday happenings within the entrepreneur-manager's projects.

Coaching and Support

Coaching is a role that is much celebrated but not often practiced, for one simple reason. Coaching takes time, and senior leaders don't have much of it. We are not going to draw up a long list of things that the leader should do as a coach. We simply look to sponsors not only to document the idea failures and ineffective behaviors of the entrepreneur-manager but also to offer counseling on how the manager can improve his skills.

A common challenge is to temper the stubbornness of the entrepreneur-manager with a more pragmatic approach. Bob Wood, a former group president at Dow Chemical, noted:

> Some entrepreneurs would rush to go from A to B, knocking down barriers, any obstacle in the way. But it takes a lot of energy to knock down obstacles. It may be smarter to go around this obstacle. That might be the more effective way to achieve results. I have to give very authentic feedback on what I see. That is the only way I can help in the rounding process of the entrepreneur. I also try to ensure that the context in which the entrepreneur functions keeps changing so that there is a new opportunity to test his/her skills.

Sponsors must also identify with the renewal project that they are sponsoring and be willing to cover for the entrepreneur-manager in dealings with top management and other business heads. This helps build trust. We saw an example of this behavior earlier in the Nespresso story. Says Camillo Pagano, a former senior executive vice president and a sponsor of the Nespresso project:

> I saw this contraption that somebody said was going to be fantastic. I discovered that the R&D team had developed this system without even really talking to the marketing side. There is no doubt that technical development can bring innovation. But internally, there was a lot of skepticism about the possibility to

commercialize Nespresso. People thought I was a nut to spend so much time on this small thing and to support the idea. Nespresso is so different from what the company does in its day-to-day business. You need champions at the top for a new idea. You need to give an idea support against criticism.

A more common task for the sponsor is smoothing the ruffled feathers that entrepreneur-managers leave in their paths. We saw an example of this earlier in the Dow Chemical venture. Philippe Raynaud de Fitte, the line boss, had the unenviable task of helping his colleagues on the division's leadership team understand why it was necessary for Telford to start the e-mail chain and produce the fake video in support of his venture. He was firmly convinced that these were distractions that risked hurting the project, but he also recognized that cutting them out completely would hurt Telford's motivation. He had to support Telford but also not hurt the project.

The entrepreneur-manager, as we noted, must borrow with pride. However, the lender might not look upon all of this borrowing favorably. When Ganev attracted five of his former colleagues to the CTS business, his boss, Ulf Mimer, had to go the Components Division, offer all the right apologies and declare that such poaching would stop.

In all of these cases, sponsors have to use the goodwill and personal credibility that they have built in the organization to support the entrepreneur-manager. This support is a vital source of motivation for the entrepreneur-manager. However, as noted earlier, the sponsor must also draw a clear line on when bending or breaking of rules will not be condoned. Violations of company values should be consistently punished. Michael Garrett, a former Nestlé executive vice president, observed:

It would have been hypocritical of me to ask for entrepreneurship and risk taking and then throw the rule book at my staff all the time. Granted that rules are there for a purpose, but at times they have to be broken. However, in supporting these "entrepreneurs," senior managers must appear to be consistent and not be seen as playing favorites.

Even when a renewal project performs spectacularly, or if the manager concerned is especially creative, there can be no favorites when core values are breached.

Summary

Behind every successful entrepreneur-manager is a strong sponsor. Sponsors are usually senior executives—regional heads, heads of business divisions and functions. They have an excellent track record of performance. That buys them credibility in the organization and influence with top management. However, they do not have to have been entrepreneur-managers themselves.

Sponsors play five important roles:

> Defining the renewal agenda
> Finding the right entrepreneur-manager to staff the project
> Locating the proper organizational home for the project
> Tailoring the control and reward systems to help implementation
> Coaching and supporting the entrepreneur-manager.

These roles are mutually reinforcing. Through these, an effective sponsor helps develop both the entrepreneur-manager and his business and enhances the commitment that the entrepreneur-manager has to the firm.

CHAPTER 7

Directing Renewal

"A big overstatement is sometimes needed in order to get the organization moving in the right direction again. But this is the beauty of managing dilemmas, isn't it? You sometimes have to appear partial toward one goal, given prior conflicts, the history of the organization and the set of characters involved."

—Daniel Vasella, chairman and CEO, Novartis

We started this book by comparing the job of top management to that of an Oscar-winning motion picture director. In fact, we believe top management is actually a far more difficult task. We devote this final chapter to the role of top management in directing renewal. As the chairman and CEO of Novartis, Dan Vasella points out this is a continuous balancing act, trading off between equally important goals while moving the organization forward.

In the previous two chapters, we discussed the important role that the entrepreneur-manager and his sponsor play in shaping and implementing the firm's renewal strategies. We noted that these strategies have to advance the firm's corporate vision. Setting this vision is the responsibility of top management. Although a new vision represents change, it is also the responsibility of top management to celebrate the thread of continuity that a firm has through its core purpose and core values. As the work of James Collins and Jerry Porras in *Built to Last*,[1] and Jim Collins in *Good to Great*,[2] clearly show, companies that achieve sustained superior performance are guided by their core purpose and core values in their renewal. Managing this tension between continuity and change is the first challenge for top management.

Another special challenge is to create a culture with the right balance between one where managers deliver on their promises and another where they cooperate and share with other units in the firm. The discipline around delivering results as promised should not lead to silo thinking inside the firm. The renewal strategies of leverage and build, in particular, count on a sharing culture for their success.

Finally, in the execution of the firm's renewal strategies, there will be the inevitable trade-offs between equally important but contending goals—dilemmas. Top management will have to use its influence and power to create the right counterbalance in support of the goal that is out of favor.

Continuity and Change

In driving renewal, top management seeks to balance the culture of change that continuous renewal brings with a sense of continuity.

Core Purpose and Values

The organization needs to feel anchored in *something;* this something is what Jim Collins and Jerry Porras call the core purpose and core values of a firm.

Core purpose defines a firm's *raison d'etre* or what the world would miss if it ceases to exist. Purpose demarcates a firm's renewal efforts, pointing both to the direction in which it should seek growth and to domains that it should not pursue. Consider Best Buy, for example; its core purpose is to bring to consumers at home and in small businesses leading-edge consumer electronics technology in a user-friendly way at the best possible price. At Nestlé, it is to make good food central to enjoying a good healthy life for consumers everywhere; and at Medtronic, the core purpose is to contribute to human welfare by application of biomedical engineering in the research, design, manufacture, and sale of instruments or appliances that alleviate pain, restore health, and extend life. These are all different and yet equally powerful. What matters is whether a core purpose gives a firm's employees a sense of pride, challenge, and direction, and not whether it is unique and phrased cleverly.

Core values, on the other hand, define the approved behaviors for a firm's employees as they strive to serve its core purpose. They provide the firm its identity, an important reason why not only the firm's employees but also its suppliers, customers, and financiers seek to affiliate with it. And, in turn, that is why its host communities grant it the license to operate. Core values, like core purpose, are important elements of a firm's employee value proposition. The more appealing these are, the easier it is to attract top talent to the company and to retain it. They also make tangible inducements such as salary and other financial benefits less salient to an employee's motivation. Simply put, an engaging core purpose and an appealing set of core values attracts voluntary contributions and superior firm performance.

The continuity that core purpose and core values provide a firm is vital to its renewal. Consider Medtronic, a company that we have described previously in this book. Medtronic executives firmly believe that its mission (see box), formulated by its founder Earl Bakken, has not only stood the company in good stead in the past, but will also be central to its growth over the next hundred years. Bill George, former CEO and chairman of the company, explained its impact:[3]

> *The Medtronic mission has created unusually high levels of employee motivation to serve our customers. This motivation has resulted in a superior record of innovation, product development, and customer service. As a direct result, Medtronic's market share has grown rapidly, as has our ability to develop new markets. We are in the business of maximizing value to the patients whom we serve. We do not chase maximizing shareholder value as a primary goal. But we haven't done too shabbily there either.*

Medtronic Mission Statement

> To contribute to human welfare by application of biomedical engineering in the research, design, manufacture, and sale of instruments or appliances that alleviate pain, restore health, and extend life.

> To direct our growth in the areas of biomedical engineering where we display maximum strength and ability; to gather people and facilities that tend to augment these areas; to continuously build on these areas through education and knowledge assimilation; to avoid participation in areas where we cannot make unique and worthy contributions.

> To strive without reserve for the greatest possible reliability and quality in our products; to be the unsurpassed standard of comparison and to be recognized as a company of dedication, honesty, integrity, and service.

> To make a fair profit on current operations to meet our obligations, sustain our growth, and reach our goals.

> To recognize the personal worth of employees by providing an employment framework that allows personal satisfaction in work accomplished, security, advancement opportunity, and means to share in the company's success.

> To maintain good citizenship as a company.

Source: Medtronic

Championing the core purpose and values of the firm is the responsibility of all its managers, but top management has to show the way. At Medtronic, a number of traditions help the mission "come to life." The first of these is the mission and medallion ceremony. Initiated by Bakken in the early 1960s, this requires the CEO to meet personally with every new employee and present him or her with a bronze medallion inscribed with the company's mission.

A second unique and important tradition is the annual Medtronic holiday party. In December every year, Medtronic invites select patients and their physicians to its headquarters in Minneapolis. Patients tell their personal healing stories to the employees and thank them for the opportunity to be restored and lead a full life. These unscripted stories are relayed to all Medtronic locations throughout the world. As Art Collins, the company's chairman and CEO, observed:

> *These stories are what I want to be remembered for ... Not the consecutive string of profitable quarters, but the material way in which Medtronic has improved the lives of millions of people ... Every five seconds, a Medtronic product saves or substantially improves a life somewhere in the world.*

The core values of Medtronic help spark innovation. The thought that these innovations can help save or substantially improve the quality of a life somewhere in the world can be a powerful motivator.

Reinventing the Company

Although core purpose and core values are important, they are not sufficient. Just as important is the continuous reinterpretation of the core purpose into meaningful visions.

As we have pointed out earlier, directing profitable growth is to recognize the inherent performance dilemmas between profitability and growth and between short- and long-term performance. These competing performance goals have to be balanced continuously.

CEOs such as Brad Anderson of Best Buy, Art Collins of Medtronic, and Peter Brabeck-Letmathe of Nestlé demand a simultaneous emphasis on profitability and growth in their firms. We described earlier the deep-rooted discipline at Medtronic to pursue both growth and profitability in all businesses of the company. In the case of Nestlé, there is a conscious attempt to separate out growth that results from exchange rate changes or through acquisitions and to focus solely on superior organic growth when compared to peers. The firm achieved a yearly organic growth of 6.2 percent in 2005, one of the highest among its peers.

But Best Buy, Medtronic, and Nestlé are firms that have a good record of sustaining profitable growth. Even in the case of companies such as Philips Electronics or ABB, which have brushed with bankruptcy in the recent past, their CEOs have emphasized a balanced pursuit of profitability and growth. We described the balanced performance metrics that Fred Kindle, its CEO, has introduced at ABB, insisting on performance against growth in orders and revenue; changes in operating margin—measured as earnings before interest and taxes (EBIT) as a percentage of revenue; and capital efficiency—measured via both return on capital employed (ROCE) and return on equity (ROE). Similarly, Gerard Kleisterlee, president of Philips, has demanded sustained profitable growth from his organization.

Corporate leaders like Kindle and Kleisterlee recognize that balance begets balance and that their firms must start on this positive spiral toward sustaining both profitability and growth. However, their task is not easy. They must not only sell their goal of balanced performance to their managers but also to their boards, which will be under pressure from analysts to stay the course of improving profitability (even at the expense of growth).

Demanding balanced performance is an important and courageous first step, but it has to be backed by a credible and energizing vision. Whether it is for transforming the company or in its continuous renewal, periodic re-visioning of the company is important.

In the case of Medtronic, the company has evolved through three successive visions over 50 years: inventing the pacemaker industry, going global and building the premier medical technology franchise, and revolutionizing chronic disease state management. Around the company, the phrase *reinventing Medtronic* is not a cliché. The company has grown from a primary focus on chronic heart disease to include other chronic diseases such as neurological disorders and diabetes. Successive leaders have initiated periodic re-visioning in response to the changing competitive environment facing the company.

We had a rich account in Chapter 3, "Continuous Renewal," of how at Best Buy the company's core purpose was repeatedly translated into new energizing visions. The company has grown successfully under six different visions, called concepts in the company's internal vocabulary. Concept I was to establish the first consumer electronics superstore in the Minneapolis market. Its primary appeal was to vanquish smaller competitors. Concept II was to transform the company into a discount warehouse. This was a defensive move to ward off predatory attacks from regional stores like Highland. Success was achieved when Highland went bankrupt. Concept III was to establish a hybrid store to sell both higher-end and commodity products under a single roof. The rationale for this was to beat the industry leader, Circuit City, in both sales and profitability. When that happened—Best Buy had vanquished its immediate competitors—it then needed a new focus.

Concepts IV and V did not have a particular competitor in sight but were aimed at complementing product sales with service and solution selling, seamlessly integrating the bricks-and-mortar store with its Web cousin and providing more modularity and flexibility to all Best Buy stores. Concept VI was skipped intentionally, and Concept VII, the customer-centric store, was announced to serve the consumer better than the company's new competitors—Wal-Mart, Amazon, and Dell.

Visions That Energize

Visions that energize are simple and short. The have to evoke an imminent threat or a highly desirable end state. They are appealing—the why is clear. The goals are tangible and can be broken down into credible milestones. Above all, they invite personal contributions from employees.

Consider Concept VII. It was about customer-centricity, "controlling the last ten feet" to the customer—knowing them better than any of Best Buy's competitors. This was necessary to counter the operational and logistical efficiencies of Wal-Mart—a competitor that grew at the rate of one Best Buy each year; the mass customization abilities of Dell—with its rapidly expanding presence in retailing consumer electronics; and the shopping convenience provided by e-retailers such as Amazon and eBay.

Above all, customer-centricity was empowering. Front-line store managers and employees were the prime drivers of this vision.

However, unlike at Best Buy, it might be hard to set a single energizing vision across multiple businesses in a diversified company. Take Royal Dutch Shell, for example. When its CEO, Jeroen van der Veer, took charge in 2004, he provided a simple mantra: "More Upstream, Profitable Downstream." When asked whether this was his vision, mission, or strategy, he smiled and responded: "It is all of those." What Van der Veer was pointing to is the need for Shell's senior managers to translate this corporate strategy (a broad portfolio choice signaling more funding for the firm's upstream businesses) into goals that are energizing for their employees. Goals that are set closer to a business are likely to be the most relevant and engaging. We suggested in Chapter 6, "Sponsoring Renewal," that setting these goals is the responsibility of senior executives in charge of these businesses.

Timing for the New Vision

Balancing the tension between continuity and change is a key challenge for the CEO as the firm's chief strategist. Jumping to a new vision prematurely can be just as detrimental to the firm's success as holding on to an existing vision that is getting stale. Dan Vasella, the chairman and CEO of Novartis, frames this challenge well. In an interview, he summarized it as follows:[4]

> *Risk taking is fun. The gambling side urges you to focus on the upside, but the prudent side cautions you from taking the company to the cleaners. Unfortunately, CEOs do not get punished for avoiding risks. But an authentic leader must be both risk taking and prudent. Otherwise you are just presiding!*

We have argued that the timing should be based on a realistic assessment of the extent to which existing markets and competencies are losing their attractiveness and new ones are emerging. But visioning is not just an analytic exercise. It is also driven by the intuition of top management. Canon's entry into photocopiers was based as much on the intuition of its senior leaders as it was on analysis. A thorough analysis would have most probably aborted the company's entry, given the worldwide dominance at that time of Xerox in photocopiers.

Every leader is a visionary, but some are able to see opportunities quicker than others and have the courage and persistence to steer their organizations toward this new vision. Imagine the resistance that Brad Anderson would have faced at Best Buy when he announced Concept VII, customer-centricity, at a time when the company had produced record profits and growth using Concept V. Or, the skepticism with which Peter Brabeck-Letmathe's push toward the growing "phood" opportunity—a space where pharmaceuticals and food intersect—must have been met with at Nestlé. It is not enough to let hindsight prove a leader right; he or she must be able to sell the new vision skillfully to all the firm's stakeholders.

Providing a Strategy Architecture

Top management must also provide the strategic architecture for driving its vision, outlining the broad emphasis that it desires across the four renewal strategies of protect and extend, leverage, build, and transform.

These strategies in turn can be executed through organic growth, acquisitions, or alliances. It is the role of top management to ensure that the right blend of means is deployed. Major acquisitions and large strategic alliances are clearly the prerogative of top management. Peter Brabeck-Letmathe at Nestlé and Art Collins at Medtronic provide great examples of how organic growth, acquisitions, and alliances can be blended successfully.

When the preference is for organic growth, we suggested in Chapter 3 that repeated leverage-build sequences can help transform the firm, but in an evolutionary fashion. This is continuous renewal. Dick Schulze and Brad Anderson at Best Buy, between the two of them, have guided the company through two decades of continuous renewal.

Championing Change

A new vision brings change to a company's internal power structure. For example, at Best Buy, in the lab stores where customer-centricity was first tested, there was a noticeable shift of power from the corporate office to the retail stores. Historically, product assortment in the stores was modified five times a year. The merchant and the general merchandise teams would meet, decide what they wanted, and communicate their decisions to the field for implementation. Local stores did not have a say in the process. With the introduction of customer-centricity they did, and on a much more regular basis.

Newcomers to Best Buy's executive team had mixed reactions to this change. Some had been brought in specifically to strengthen corporate functions. For example, under the customer-centric approach, lab stores were given control over their advertising budget. A direct consequence of the lab stores' autonomy was a sudden inflow of new ideas, not all of them brilliantly thought through. Mike Linton, the chief marketing officer, confessed that his team, which had been trying to strengthen the marketing discipline within the company, took a while to adapt to the new reality: The resistance was higher among old-timers. Mike Keskey, the then-head of retail for Best Buy, acknowledged candidly:

> *Without Brad, we wouldn't be doing it because it is so hard. In order to make the customer the king or queen, whoever is closest to the customer has to be the new royalty. Just think of the implications, changes in the locus of power within the organization, people and systems implications, customer implications, and above all investor implications. I'll be very honest. Initially I was fighting it. But I'm glad that Brad persisted. It took me probably four months to see the merits of the customer-centric approach.*

Brad Anderson, the company's CEO, had to shift the power pendulum away from corporate executives more toward mid-level managers in the field and in the stores. He began giving these managers more of a voice in key corporate decisions. It took a while for the initial resistance to ease. Anderson remarked at that time:

> *When you are as successful as we have been recently, there is a tendency for the organization to be bogged down in the status quo. The CEO has the responsibility to shake the organization out of its complacency. I am dispassionate, like to study things and get a broader view before I am ready to announce a change. But once I am convinced, I have learned an important skill from our founder, Schulze. I will go through the wall, if necessary. That is what I am doing now.*

Top management has to be the chief change champion when advocating a new vision.

Selling Growth to External Stakeholders

Big companies have had a lot of bad press over recent years.
Anticapitalist protests, boycotts, and campaigns tend to focus on
the world's largest corporations as exemplars of all that is bad in
the capitalist world. Somehow being big is also seen as being bad.

It is true that of the 100 largest economies in the world at
the turn of this century, 51 were corporations.[5] It is equally true
that in many global industries, remaining competitive demands
that companies be of a certain size. Consider, for example, BP,
Exxon-Mobil, and Royal Dutch Shell in the energy sector; AXA,
Allianz, and Citigroup in the financial services sector; NTT, IBM,
Deutsche Telekom, and HP in the information and
communications sector; General Motors, Daimler Chrysler,
and Toyota in the auto sector; and more recently, Wal-Mart,
Carrefour, and Metro in the retail sector. They are big and need
to be.

What is more important than a company's absolute size is its
relative size vis-à-vis its industry peers. There are well-established
laws to deal with monopolistic and other anticompetitive
practices. Leaders of large firms need not abandon the pursuit of
profitable growth but must recognize the growing public
sentiment against them and work hard to show that profitable
growth is not just good for the firm's shareholders but also for its
other stakeholders. However, a recent survey by McKinsey &
Company shows that only one in seven executives in top
management believed he played a leadership role in addressing
sociopolitical issues.

It is clear that most firms will strive to create value for their
shareholders. At the same time, the firm must also function more
broadly, as part of society. Growth is good for employees because
of the added job opportunities that it brings. Host communities
support growth because it benefits them directly through higher
tax incomes and indirectly through other trickle-down benefits to

their economies. The firm's customers and suppliers should rejoice in the stability that its growth can bring to the transactions with them. Growth can help improve the legitimacy of the firm and strengthen its "license to operate."

Social pressures will always be there and must be handled with integrity. As Dan Vasella of Novartis says, a good leader should probably never be afraid of what is being reported in the media the next day. For him, decisions must be made in such a way that social pressure and shareholder value creation are dealt with in a win-win mentality! Novartis naturally focuses on strong value creation for its shareholders It seeks to develop innovative new drugs, which will enjoy a number of years of patent protection and yield healthy returns on the billions of dollars invested in their development. At the same time, as a drug company, Novartis cannot forget its responsibility to deal with human pain and suffering. It has initiated special programs for supporting poor patients. Vasella notes with pride:

> *Last year, taking all pro bono contributions into account, the total aid Novartis provided for patients in need amounted to $696 million, with 6.5 million patients being treated. The main element of this commitment was the donation of medicines for the treatment of leprosy, malaria, tuberculosis, and chronic myeloid leukemia.*

On the flip side, the challenge for corporate leaders is to pursue only those growth initiatives that can be sustained profitably, regardless of the appeal of individual initiatives to different stakeholders. Quoting Winston Churchill, Vasella captures the political reality that confronts corporate leaders:

> *Some regard private enterprise as if it were a predatory tiger to be shot. Others look upon it as a cow that they can milk. Only a handful see it for what it really is: the strong horse that pulls the whole cart.*

Accountability and Sharing

Accountability is a magic mantra in firms today. It simply means that every manager must be disciplined to deliver against his or her budgeted commitments. Enterprise-first thinking is the other mantra. It urges the various organizational units in the firm's matrix to share with each other and do what is best for the firm. However, sharing is difficult, made more so by the growing scrutiny over the performance of individual organizational units. The challenge is to have both accountability and sharing.

Senior staff executives will surely assist in achieving this balance, but only if top management sees the need for it. Gerard Kleisterlee's efforts at promoting sharing within Philips, Jeroen van der Veer's passion around enterprise-first behaviors at Shell, and Brad Anderson's commitment to unleash human creativity at Best Buy remind us of the important role that top management plays in promoting sharing. Accountability should not drive out teamwork. Both leverage and build strategies rely heavily on cross-business and cross-functional sharing. Organizational units should enjoy autonomy and yet remain connected to each other. Only then can they take advantage of all of the firm's competencies and market knowledge.

Paradoxically, the very features of a competence that make it distinctive and hard for competitors to procure or copy are also the ones that make it difficult for it to be leveraged by other businesses within the firm. For example, know-how that is not fully articulated in "how to" manuals can be protected more easily from competitors, but transferring it internally is difficult, too. Tacit knowledge is best transferred through apprenticeship with the donor business. However, this places a disproportionate time and cost burden on the teacher rather than on the student. The donor division is often not the beneficiary of the growth that follows.

In our own research, we have found that cross-business sharing requires opportunities and motivation. Creating a sharing culture requires the direct intervention of top management. It intervenes by creating more opportunities for sharing and by providing a real incentive for sharing.

Creating Opportunities for Sharing

The drive to meet performance targets is so intense that business managers seldom look beyond their own silos. To leverage competencies across businesses, however, it is important to know where these are. In companies such as 3M or Nestlé, the corporate technology group arranges periodic meetings to ensure that there is cross-business sharing of the company's technology developments. But technology is not the only competence that can be leveraged. Nucor Steel, in its heyday, was famous for encouraging its employees to visit high-performing plants and appreciate the state of the art in manufacturing practices. Sharing happens if there are opportunities for frequent contacts across businesses at multiple levels in the organization and across functions.

A well-planned job-rotation program between a company's businesses and functions can help in this regard. At Sharp,[6] top management insists that job rotation be reserved for the company's top performers and not for those who can be "spared." The company actively seeks to rotate its technical and commercial people across businesses and functions to encourage such "chemicalization" (mixing of diverse talent to create a new business idea).

We also discussed in the preceding chapter how top management helps renewal by creating standalone subsidiaries and new venture organizations and by sponsoring corporate projects. These are helpful arrangements for promoting sharing through their use of cross-business and cross-functional teams.

Although job rotation and cross-business/functional teams are the most effective ways of creating opportunities for sharing, information systems can also help. Nestlé has completed a project called GLOBE (Global Business Excellence).[7] One of its objectives is to identify and codify best practices and share these throughout Nestlé. The challenge here is to recognize that codified knowledge not only flows more easily within the firm but can also leak out. Moreover, all knowledge cannot be codified. Therefore, some organizations, such as the consulting firm McKinsey & Company, have chosen to list their experts (and not just their expertise) on the intranet. These internal experts are important guides for accessing a firm's distinctive know-how and skills.

Nurturing the Motivation to Share

We discussed earlier the role of top management in championing the firm's core purpose and core values. An important benefit of that is to promote better sharing within the firm.

Sharing happens if the members of an organization are predisposed to share. A shared core purpose is an important driver for sharing opportunities and competencies. For example, at Medtronic, its shared mission helps sharing across its businesses dealing with cardiology, neurology, or any other chronic disease states. There is a shared purpose of saving or substantially improving human life.

The motivation to share is also influenced by the rewards and sanctions that a firm provides. Ideally, the reward system must provide bonuses that are based not just on the performance of a business but also on the broader cluster to which it belongs. This promotes sharing. What is even more effective is when sharing becomes a key requirement for career advancement within a company. Royal Dutch Shell, under the leadership of its CEO Jeroen van der Veer, has defined what it calls enterprise-first behaviors. Van der Veer is seeking to build a mindset where "everybody is like a wheel in a Swiss clock; the wheels are all different, but all are essential for performance." A key behavior that underlies enterprise-first, besides leadership and accountability, is teamwork. Van der Veer expects greater cooperation and sharing between the company's businesses, and career consequences apply at all levels for not conforming.

The most powerful motivation for sharing is organizational culture. George Buckley, the current chairman, president, and CEO of 3M notes: "A few formal processes exist for sharing technology, but the real process is the informal network of engineers and scientists. Sharing your ideas is celebrated at 3M." He goes on to add: "Giant egos are not welcomed at 3M, and they generally don't survive in our company. We value modesty, honesty, and industriousness in our people. We value individual creativity, but we value teamwork equally." The core values of 3M are the glue that promotes sharing and teamwork in the company.

Managing Dilemmas

As we have discussed throughout this book, whether it is performance, strategy, people management, or organization, there are inherent tensions that have to be managed. What Novartis's Dan Vasella and other successful corporate leaders have mastered is the fine art of continuously balancing seemingly conflicting values—*dilemmas.* There are two simple lessons that they offer: (1) Dilemmas are increasingly a part of corporate life—enjoy and even celebrate them; and (2) managing dilemmas is to rectify an imbalance between the attention paid to competing goals, so the weight of top management's influence and power should be directed toward the neglected or "unchosen" goal.

Celebrating Dilemmas

Effective leaders see the pull of multiple objectives as not only good for their firms but also for their own leadership. Dan Vasella has written about the many challenges that he faced in overseeing the development of a drug called Gleevec.[8] It is a wonder drug to fight a life-threatening form of blood cancer called chronic myeloid leukemia (CML).

As the head of Novartis, with a mission to discover and develop drug therapies that will help prolong, improve, or even save the lives of patients, Vasella felt pressured to bring Gleevec to the market despite its limited commercial potential. He writes:

> *After all, who could forget the lives of patients were at stake? What we really cared about were all the patients who were waiting for a better, safer and more effective drug.*

He also notes that discovering this drug was a high point for the drug R&D team (a chance in a lifetime as some saw it). Aborting its launch could have seriously damaged the morale of the company's scientists. He states:

> *It is my duty to help create a fertile environment for drug discovery and development by choosing and supporting the right scientists: those who take calculated risks, who are dedicated to our mission; they should also have aspirations and be superb professionals.*

And yet, the goal of a decent return to Novartis stockholders could not be ignored either. Vasella observes:

> *If it were purely a personal choice, we would ignore the questions that business professionals must ask. We would avoid asking how many patients suffer from CML. We would not ask whether we could supply this drug without charging a high price. We would not ask what would be the costs to the other parts of our business, if we threw large amounts of capital and human resources into the development and manufacturing of this drug. We would skip all those questions. But we cannot for, as I said, we are a business.*

Successful leaders see the pursuit of multiple goals as healthy. As the head of a leading pharmaceuticals company, Vasella needs the passion and creativity of his scientists. He also has to satisfy the firm's shareholders, while living up to the company's values of alleviating human pain and suffering. Which goal could he choose not to serve any way? Dilemmas would indeed disappear if one of these goals was made paramount, but then the challenge of leadership would diminish, too.

Caring for the Unchosen

The Gleevec example is helpful in illustrating an important leadership principle. Effective leaders must use the power and influence that they carry in the organization to better balance competing goals. When Dan Vasella became CEO of Novartis in 1996, he was concerned that the company was losing its scientific edge. The new drug pipeline was running low. One of his early priorities was to stimulate the company's enormous but relatively dormant talent for new drug discovery. So, when he first heard about the potential therapeutic power of Gleevec, he saw in the project a chance to pump new energy into his scientific team. He told his technical team, "Money doesn't matter. Let's just do it." And when the head of development complained that he didn't have enough drug substance to manufacture the drug, Vasella simply told him "Just make it."

When we later asked Vasella why he pushed Gleevec so hard, despite his concerns over its financial viability or the technical and regulatory risks involved, he simply said:

> *I was confronted with people bringing up 101 reasons why we couldn't develop this drug and that there was no market for it. I decided to push it.*

> *A big overstatement is sometimes needed in order to get the organization moving in the right direction again. But this is the beauty of managing dilemmas, isn't it? You sometimes have to appear partial toward one goal, given prior conflicts, the history of the organization and the set of characters involved.*

In managing dilemmas, the leaders must have a clear sense of the goal that is not getting the attention that it deserves and then place the weight of their influence and power in the corner behind those who can champion this goal. As Vasella points out, it is easy to lean in the direction of normal human emotion:

> *People understand and support a lot when you act in a way which corresponds to normal human values, which is to show compassion and empathy with the patients and their families who are suffering. Creating novel medicines and not pushing for profits appeals to most human beings. And so when I say money doesn't play a role in the Gleevec example, they are able to understand that.*

In other instances, if the leader wants to push better profitability (after all, that is the fuel that sparks investment in research), it might be a harder sell. But that, too, is caring for the unchosen.

The strategy, organization, or people management goal that is receiving less attention within the organization is the one that needs championing. Its advocates are the ones who need encouragement. This might make the leader appear inconsistent, favoring the champions of one goal at times and the competing goal at other times. Pulling off these apparent two-faced acts without compromising authenticity is the hallmark of an effective leader.

Summary

Sydney Pollack, the Oscar-winning movie director and producer, is quoted as having said the following:

> *The things people always talk about in an interview about leadership aren't the things that are the most difficult or the most interesting about leadership: They're the more tangible things.*[9]

The more tangible roles of top management are setting the strategic context and driving execution. These are important, but perhaps the most difficult and interesting aspects of leadership are balancing continuity and change; accountability and sharing; and managing the associated dilemmas in these and other trade-offs that have to be made in the renewal journey. And these, too, as we have discovered, are vital elements in achieving the demanding task of sustaining profitable growth.

Epilogue

CHAPTER 8

The Multiactor Process

I have always believed the social system is the most significant competitive advantage that a company can have. Social system and culture are crucial for delivering a new strategy.

—Bradbury (Brad) Anderson, Vice Chairman and CEO, Best Buy

We started this book with the task of answering two questions: *Why is profitable growth so elusive? And, what can—and must— executives do better to drive profitable growth?* In this concluding chapter, we pull together the answers that we provide in this book.

Renewal Strategies

Sustaining profitable growth is difficult because firms fail to renew themselves continuously. As discussed in Chapter 2, "Renewal Strategies," markets that the firm competes in will mature, drying up its growth opportunities, and the competencies that it is distinctive in will over time be procured, imitated, and substituted by their competitors. We suggested that there are four renewal strategies (see Figure 8.1) the firm can use: protect and extend, leverage, build, and transform. We described each strategy at length in Chapter 2.

The two traditional strategies are protect and extend and transform. Protecting and extending the present core (the markets that the firm participates in and the distinctive competencies that it currently has) is the obvious first renewal strategy. The other strategy, transform, is to proactively migrate to new markets likely to be attractive in the future and acquire new competencies to lead in these markets.

Between these two extremes of protecting and extending the core and transforming it, we propose two other renewal strategies, leverage and build, that bridge these two. Leverage is a strategy that takes the firm to new markets by leveraging the competencies that it already has. Build is a strategy that brings new distinctive competencies to the firm to protect its existing market franchise. Both leverage and build should logically lead to the other. If the two are linked systematically, they can help the firm migrate to new markets and new competence platforms progressively over time.

The four renewal strategies can benefit from acquisitions, alliances, and organic growth. You saw an example of a firm, Medtronic, in Chapter 4, "A Blended Approach," that has successfully used a blend of all these approaches to renew itself continuously. Although acquisitions and alliances can provide growth platforms, organic growth is the primary vehicle for renewal. We saw this at Medtronic and also at Nestlé. In Chapter 3, "Continuous Renewal," you saw another example of a firm, Best Buy, that has renewed itself primarily through the use of an organic growth strategy. The essence of its approach is a continuous sequence of leverage and build initiatives.

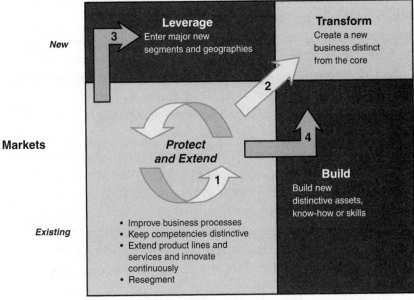

Figure 8.1
Four renewal strategies.

Formulating the right blend of strategies is an important first step. However, as Brad Anderson notes the quality of the process used to deliver them is the real source of a firm's competitive advantage.

Entrepreneur-Manager

Clearly, the entrepreneur-manager is critical to the renewal efforts of the firm, especially in executing its leverage, build, and transform strategies. We profiled such a manager in Chapter 5. This is not to suggest that maintaining the health of the current businesses, and protecting and extending their scope, is unimportant. In fact, as we have acknowledged in the book, this should rightfully be the predominant concern of the company's leaders. Our purpose here in highlighting the entrepreneur-manager's role is to focus attention on renewal, a neglected agenda in many firms. To repeat a phrase we coined in Chapter 7, "Directing Renewal," continuous renewal requires caring for the "unchosen." The entrepreneur-manager is the unchosen one in many of our firms.

Let's start with the central figure, entrepreneur-managers (see Figure 8.2).[1] As we described in Chapter 5, they are not special managers, but are instead good operating managers with a few special traits: propensity for risk taking, action oriented, passionate and high energy, and self-confident. These are not traits that are explicitly sought (perhaps they should be) in the hiring process, but neither does the hiring process explicitly exclude individuals with these traits. There are plenty of budding entrepreneur-managers in the company, certainly enough to drive its renewal projects. The problem, however, is that these budding entrepreneur-managers are not always spotted or assigned to the right renewal projects.

It is the responsibility of the senior executive sponsor to spot the entrepreneur-manager, assign a project that is suited to his skill level and aspiration, and attach it to a standalone subsidiary, new venture organization, or special project—depending on the autonomy and connectedness that the project needs. We discussed these aspects at length in Chapter 6, "Sponsoring Renewal."

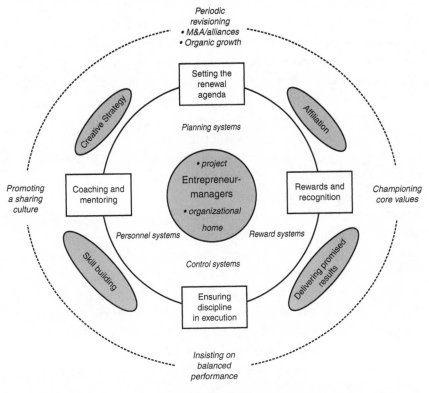

Figure 8.2
Supporting the entrepreneur-manager.

When this is done, the entrepreneur-manager has an organizational home and an exciting project to manage. He is now ready for action but will need guidance and support. The support we recommend is shown in Figure 8.2 by the two rings. The inner ring represents the role of the sponsor, and the outer ring (in dotted line) that of top management.

The Sponsor's Role

We discussed the sponsor's role in Chapter 6. The sponsor sets the renewal agenda for the entrepreneur-manager's project, laying out its broad scope. The interactions and iterations in the goal setting and strategy development process have to be tailored to suit the risk involved in the project . The entrepreneur-manager has to channel his creative energies toward the agreed-upon goal.

The sponsor also adapts the firm's budgeting system to distinguish between delivering renewal and maintaining the current momentum of a business. This distinction is important for several reasons. First, the funding for a renewal project has to be fenced so that it is not drained off to fight operational problems. Second, it has to be monitored differently. Savings against a renewal budget may not be any cause for celebration. It may be because of project delays, not project savings. Finally, high-risk renewal projects need to proceed through trial and error. Each step of this process can encounter failure. Prudent risk taking requires a monitoring of the quality of effort expended by the entrepreneur-manager. Waiting for the final project outcome might be too late. The project may need mid-course corrections or even abandonment.

Both during strategy development and execution, the entrepreneur-manager must be coached and mentored (and given political support by the sponsor). As discussed in Chapter 5, a renewal project has to be communicated and marketed skillfully. It may also face resistance from internal stakeholders. These have to be overcome with patience and sensitivity. In executing the project, the entrepreneur-manager may face additional hurdles, too. At each step, the coaching and support of the sponsor is vital, not only for the success of the project but also for the development of the entrepreneur-manager.

The sponsor must also recognize and reward the entrepreneur-manager in a timely fashion. Timely recognition is actually harder than handing out performance bonuses. The sponsor must have intimate knowledge of those actions of an entrepreneur-manager that are deserving of praise and find the right forum to give prompt and public recognition. Recognition delayed is recognition denied. Incentive bonuses, by contrast, can be delayed and processed through the anonymity of the firm's bureaucracy.

The four key roles of the sponsor are shown in the four boxes in the inner ring, around the entrepreneur-manager, in Figure 8.2.

Support of Staff Executives

Next to each sponsoring role (the four boxes) is the management system (planning, control, reward, and personnel) that is most salient to it. These systems are designed and administered by senior staff executives. The problem, however, is that the designs are often influenced by wanting to be best in class, and not to be fit for purpose. Also, the systems may be misaligned with each other. It is rare to have the planning, control, and human resource management experts in a firm jointly design its management systems. It is rarer still for senior business executives or top management to get involved in this process. As a senior business executive noted: "Design of management systems is too important a task to be left solely to the systems experts in the company."

Our purpose in noting the four systems in Figure 8.2 is to urge senior staff executives to consider whether the systems that they provide encourage an entrepreneur-manager to be creative and take prudent risks. Are these appropriate to the renewal agenda that he has been assigned? An integrative planning system or a budgeting system that only supports maintaining current momentum, an incentive system that is solely tied to bottom-line performance, or a personnel system that discourages job rotation may severely constrain entrepreneurial behaviors and hence business renewal.

We made a few suggestions in Chapter 6 about how these systems can be tailored to support renewal strategies.

Top Management Support

The outer ring (dotted line) in Figure 8.2 denotes the intervention that top management provides. As you saw in Chapter 7, an energizing vision is an important trigger for renewal, as is top management's insistence on balance between profitability and growth in every business. As we described in Chapter 1 of this book, "The Performance Dilemmas,"a strict discipline around balanced performance helps renewal.

Championing of the core values by top management can be another spark for innovation. Top management's commitment to serve the company's people, social, and environmental obligations is a source of motivation to the entrepreneur-manager. The difficult trade-off between these and the commitment to serve the company's shareholders can be framed as opportunities for innovation. You saw an example of this at Medtronic in Chapter 4, when it presented the need to serve the Chinese market as an important social cause. Its engineers came up with a low-cost pacemaker that made the venture profitable, too.

Finally, the entrepreneur-manager needs to borrow resources of the firm that fall beyond his direct authority to progress his projects. This can happen only if there is a culture of sharing within the company. Promoting such a culture is the responsibility of top management.

Top management needs to ensure that the multiple actors discussed here—the entrepreneur-manager, his sponsor, and senior executives who are responsible for the firm's management systems—can work in concert. It is this coordinated effort that helps the entrepreneur-manager come up with creative strategies without taking undue risks (and to exercise the discipline necessary to deliver the promised results).

The Outcomes

An energizing vision communicated with passion by top management and translated into a challenging renewal agenda by the sponsor increases the affiliation of the entrepreneur-manager with the firm. Recall from Chapter 5, the entrepreneur-manager is always looking for a fresh challenge, a new stretch goal. In addition, if the company's reward and recognition system treats the entrepreneur-manager fairly, his affiliation with the firm grows. Also, a firm's core values are perhaps the reason why the entrepreneur-manager joined the firm in the first place. When top management champions these values, it heightens the sense of identity that an entrepreneur-manager has with the firm. Higher affiliation is a prerequisite to entrepreneurship. To be creative on its behalf, the entrepreneur-manager must care about the firm.

Results delivery is primarily helped by a fair control system that makes it possible to deliver against both growth and profitability goals. Commensurate rewards and recognition enhance the motivation to perform and deliver results as promised.

Strict discipline is also helpful in the personal development of the entrepreneur-manager. Both failures in his own effort and flaws in the strategy that he drives must be highlighted. These are essential for learning and skill building. However, this feedback also has to be backed by supportive coaching and mentoring.

Finally, a stretch goal together with active coaching is the right combination to help the entrepreneur-manager think outside the box, come up with creative strategies, and take prudent risks.

Business renewal is helped when the entrepreneur-manager comes up with creative strategies and delivers the promised results. Higher affiliation of the entrepreneur-manager to the firm ensures continued effort, and the skills that he is able to build help in launching more ambitious renewal projects for the firm. Successful execution of renewal strategies is inextricably linked to the development of entrepreneur-managers.

Summary

As we have shown, continuous renewal is a multiactor process. Managers at each level in the organization can contribute to this process. However, each has to play his role *and* coordinate it with others. We hope the ideas and examples presented in this book inspire you in your own efforts.
Good luck!

Appendixes

APPENDIX A

The Empirical Study

Data

The data for this study was drawn from several sources:

1.   Thomson Financial and Worldscope: A company was
     selected if it was public, active, non-ADR, and with sales in
     2004 above $500 million. The sample was identified by a
     search of the Thomson One Banker Companies module.
     The full sample consists of 5,910 global firms, listed on
     major financial exchanges throughout the world.

     > We include subsidiaries that are listed as separate
       companies on local exchanges. For example, we include
       Nestlé (Malaysia) Berhad and Nestlé India Limited, two
       related companies of Nestlé SA in the sample. Locally
       focused companies might demonstrate profitability and
       growth patterns that are different from their parents.

     > The study covers 15 years, from 1990 through 2004, 11
       consecutive five-year periods. If there were missing
       values for any single year in the five-year period, we
       report the item missing for that period.

2.   We used the Industrial Classification Benchmark subsector
     (www.icbenchmark.com) to assign each firm to 1 of 104
     industry subsectors.

3.   The M&A deals were identified by a search of the Thomson
     One Banker Deals module. In this research, we built a
     universal M&A database of 338,524 deals completed from
     January 1, 1980 to April 26, 2005. During this period, there
     were 160,187 M&A deals with deal values available in the
     database. For each year from 1990 to 2004, we matched
     each of the 5,910 companies in the sample with the acquirer
     in the deals. The total number of deals completed by the
     sample firms was 31,469, and the total deal value was $9,957
     billion.

About half of the deals completed did not report deal value and so were excluded in the analysis. In addition, during the study period, some companies changed names, which could not be matched with the deals they completed. Although we managed to identify 31,469 deals, the mismatch might exclude deals for certain companies.

Measures

Profitability was measured by return on invested capital (ROIC). ROIC is defined as the cash rate of return on capital that a company has invested. Among all the alternative measures, such as return on equity, return on assets, and return on sales, ROIC is a true metric that measures the cash-on-cash yield of a firm and how effectively it allocates capital.

Return on Invested Capital =

$$\frac{\text{Net Income before Preferred Dividends +} \ [\text{(Interest Expense on Debt - Interest Capitalized)}^*(\text{1-Tax Rate})]}{\text{Last Year's Total Capital + Last Year's Short Term Debt + Current Portion of Long Term Debt}}$$

The *numerator,* net operating profit after taxes, measures the cash generated by operating activities. The measure excludes items such as income from investment, goodwill, or interest expense, which are non-operating in nature. The *denominator,* invested capital, represents all the cash that debt holders and shareholders have invested in a firm. We obtained ROIC data directly from Thomson Financial. Annual ROIC was averaged over a five-year period to get the five-year average ROIC.

Growth was measured by the annual growth rate in net sales or revenue (measured in U.S. dollars).

$$\text{Sales one year growth rate} = \left[\frac{\text{Current Year's Net Sales or Revenues}}{\text{Last Year's Total Net Sales or Revenues}} - 1 \right] \times 100$$

The yearly sales growth rate measured in U.S. dollars was directly obtained from Thomson Financial. Annual growth rate (AGR) was averaged over a five-year period to get the five-year average AGR.

Financial market performance was measured using TSR (total shareholder return). The yearly TSR is directly available from Thomson for the study period.

Organic growth intensity was measured as follows:

$$\text{Organic Growth Intensity (\%)} = \left[\frac{\text{Capital Expenditures} + \text{R \& D Expenditures over 5 years}}{\text{Sum of total revenues over the same 5-year period}} \right] \times 100$$

Acquisition intensity measures the M&A volume relative to the size of the acquirers. We define acquisition intensity as follows:

$$\text{Acquisition intensity} = \frac{\text{Sum of total deal values over a five - year period}}{\text{Sum of total revenues over the same 5 - year period}}$$

Performance Relative to Subsector

> If a firm's five-year average sales growth rate (AGR) is higher than its subsector's weighted average in the same period, it is defined as a *sustained growth company*.
> If a firm's five-year average ROIC is higher than its subsector's weighted average in the same period, it is defined as a *sustained profitable company*.

Subsector's Weighted Average AGR and ROIC

A simple average of growth rate of all firms in the subsector disregards the size effects. The weighted mean corrects the influence of high growth rate of smaller firms. For each year from 1990 to 2004, we calculated subsector weighted average AGR and ROIC. If the number of companies in the subsector is smaller than 15, the subsector and associated companies are deleted from the sample.

The weighted average AGR for a subsector for any given year was calculated as follows:

$$\text{Subsector weighted average} = \frac{\sum_{i=1}^{n} w_i x_i}{\sum_{i=1}^{n} w_i}$$

Where $x_1, x_2, \ldots, x_n$ are the annual sales growth rate (AGR) for that year for the n firms in that subsector, and

Where $w_1, w_2, \ldots, w_n$ are the corresponding firm revenues in U.S. dollars.

The weighted average ROIC for the subsector was calculated using a similar weighting procedure.

Firm Orientation

In any given five-year period, each firm can be classified into one of four orientations: sustained profitable growth, sustained profitability only, sustained growth only, and neither.

Performance Across Subsectors

Performance Record for the Period 2000–2004 Across Major Subsectors

ICB Sector or Supersector	ICB code	ICB Subsector	Number of Firms in Subsector	Profitability Only	Growth Only	Profitable Growth	Neither	Weighted Average ROIC (%)	Weigted Average AGR (%)
Oil & Gas Producers	533	Exploration & Production	63	25.40%	14.29%	25.40%	34.92%	12.53	31.35
	537	Integrated Oil & Gas	54	35.19%	14.81%	11.11%	38.89%	15.43	27.29
			117	29.91%	14.53%	18.80%	36.75%	13.98	29.32
Oil Equipment, Services & Distribution	573	Oil Equipment & Services	48	22.92%	10.42%	50.00%	16.67%	4.72	18.57
	577	Pipelines	20	45.00%	10.00%	15.00%	30.00%	6.30	55.29
			68	29.41%	10.29%	39.71%	20.59%	5.51	36.93
Chemicals	1353	Commodity Chemicals	76	13.16%	13.16%	27.63%	46.05%	6.76	15.66
	1357	Specialty Chemicals	141	19.86%	12.77%	30.50%	36.88%	4.91	9.13
			217	17.51%	12.90%	29.49%	40.09%	5.84	12.40
Basic Resources	1737	Paper	43	25.58%	6.98%	30.23%	37.21%	4.31	10.77
	1755	Nonferrous Metals	33	21.21%	6.06%	39.39%	33.33%	3.88	15.75
	1757	Steel	136	17.65%	11.03%	30.88%	40.44%	7.56	18.92
	1775	General Mining	15	20.00%	20.00%	6.67%	53.33%	12.17	32.73
			227	19.82%	10.13%	30.40%	39.65%	6.98	19.54
Construction & Materials	2353	Building Materials & Fixtures	138	23.91%	9.42%	29.71%	36.96%	5.83	11.72
	2357	Heavy Construction	168	13.69%	7.14%	26.79%	52.38%	6.12	13.49
			306	18.30%	8.17%	28.10%	45.42%	5.98	12.61
Industrial Goods & Services	2713	Aerospace	26	11.54%	26.92%	34.62%	26.92%	9.89	8.11
	2717	Defense	23	21.74%	8.70%	47.83%	21.74%	6.96	17.48
	2723	Containers & Packaging	50	26.00%	14.00%	22.00%	38.00%	4.55	11.07
	2727	Diversified Industrials	67	26.87%	20.90%	17.91%	34.33%	6.07	9.14
	2733	Electrical Components & Equipment	121	42.15%	4.13%	21.49%	32.23%	3.39	13.51
	2737	Electronic Equipment	56	10.71%	33.93%	25.00%	30.36%	6.26	8.09
	2753	Commercial Vehicles & Trucks	72	25.00%	8.33%	27.78%	38.89%	4.97	11.87
	2757	Industrial Machinery	143	15.38%	9.79%	41.96%	32.87%	4.10	7.09
	2773	Marine Transportation	41	19.51%	12.20%	29.27%	39.02%	8.51	14.69
	2777	Transportation Services	42	19.05%	4.76%	23.81%	52.38%	7.05	19.17
	2779	Trucking	28	25.00%	3.57%	17.86%	53.57%	7.04	13.28
	2791	Business Support Services	87	16.09%	26.44%	16.09%	41.38%	11.77	14.12
	2793	Business Training & Employment Agencies	24	16.67%	20.83%	20.83%	41.67%	5.42	12.45
	2797	Industrial Suppliers	45	6.67%	24.44%	57.78%	11.11%	2.86	1.81
			825	21.82%	14.67%	28.48%	35.03%	6.35	11.56
Automobiles & Parts	3353	Automobiles	44	6.82%	11.36%	59.09%	22.73%	5.40	7.83
	3355	Auto Parts	113	25.66%	7.96%	40.71%	25.66%	3.48	10.46
	3357	Tires	21	28.57%	4.76%	33.33%	33.33%	4.80	8.58
			178	21.35%	8.43%	44.38%	25.84%	4.56	8.95
Food & Beverage	3535	Distillers & Vintners	15	6.67%	46.67%	26.67%	20.00%	11.10	6.10
	3537	Soft Drinks	26	7.69%	34.62%	11.54%	46.15%	14.80	7.68
	3573	Farming & Fishing	36	33.33%	5.56%	22.22%	38.89%	5.30	15.41
	3577	Food Products	192	15.10%	18.75%	20.31%	45.83%	9.19	10.41
			269	16.36%	20.07%	20.07%	43.49%	10.10	9.90
Personal & Household Goods	3722	Durable Household Products	55	21.82%	14.55%	18.18%	45.45%	8.96	9.20
	3726	Furnishings	26	15.38%	7.69%	30.77%	46.15%	10.17	9.04
	3728	Home Construction	54	20.37%	7.41%	44.44%	27.78%	10.49	17.69
	3743	Consumer Electronics	22	18.18%	22.73%	31.82%	27.27%	3.73	9.03
	3745	Recreational Products	37	10.81%	21.62%	35.14%	32.43%	7.65	10.95
	3747	Toys	12	8.33%	25.00%	25.00%	41.67%	10.96	10.96
	3763	Clothing & Accessories	82	14.63%	18.29%	26.83%	40.24%	8.17	10.51
	3767	Personal Products	27	14.81%	37.04%	7.41%	40.74%	18.47	7.47
	3785	Tobacco	19	10.53%	21.05%	42.11%	26.32%	16.78	7.47
			334	16.17%	17.66%	29.04%	37.13%	10.60	10.26

Sector	Code	Subsector							
Health Care	4533	Health Care Providers	57	8.77%	26.32%	24.56%	40.35%	13.59	13.97
	4535	Medical Equipment	35	17.14%	22.86%	22.86%	37.14%	16.95	13.19
	4537	Medical Supplies	17	17.65%	11.76%	41.18%	29.41%	11.18	8.98
	4577	Pharmaceuticals	78	10.26%	33.33%	10.26%	46.15%	19.46	13.28
			187	11.76%	27.27%	19.79%	41.18%	15.29	12.35
Retail	5333	Drug Retailers	24	37.50%	8.33%	20.83%	33.33%	11.95	22.07
	5337	Food Retailers & Wholesalers	108	10.19%	18.52%	23.15%	48.15%	8.80	11.26
	5371	Apparel Retailers	65	6.15%	26.15%	24.62%	43.08%	15.67	10.65
	5373	Broadline Retailers	95	13.68%	17.89%	28.42%	40.00%	8.11	9.71
	5375	Home Improvement Retailers	28	14.29%	35.71%	10.71%	39.29%	15.19	15.37
	5377	Specialized Consumer Services	20	10.00%	5.00%	55.00%	30.00%	6.92	11.56
	5379	Specialty Retailers	126	16.67%	18.25%	20.63%	44.44%	10.36	13.31
			466	13.73%	19.31%	24.25%	42.70%	11.00	13.42
Media	5553	Broadcasting & Entertainment	50	62.00%	12.00%	14.00%	12.00%	-1.98	26.36
	5555	Media Agencies	18	22.22%	16.67%	27.78%	33.33%	10.52	14.63
	5557	Publishing	62	29.03%	20.97%	17.74%	32.26%	8.46	8.55
			130	40.77%	16.92%	17.69%	24.62%	5.67	16.51
Travel & Leisure	5751	Airlines	42	26.19%	4.76%	52.38%	16.67%	0.65	8.47
	5752	Gambling	31	16.13%	9.68%	6.45%	67.74%	14.80	33.02
	5753	Hotels	30	10.00%	33.33%	33.33%	23.33%	5.54	6.62
	5755	Recreational Services	14	14.29%	7.14%	14.29%	64.29%	6.95	20.97
	5757	Restaurants & Bars	53	24.53%	26.42%	20.75%	28.30%	9.86	11.23
	5759	Travel & Tourism	42	38.10%	7.14%	19.05%	35.71%	3.15	11.87
			212	23.58%	15.57%	25.94%	34.91%	6.82	15.36
Telecommunications	6535	Fixed Line Telecommunications	76	26.32%	30.26%	21.05%	22.37%	6.03	11.58
	6575	Mobile Telecommunications	48	25.00%	22.92%	25.00%	27.08%	7.68	30.71
			124	25.81%	27.42%	22.58%	24.19%	6.85	21.15
Utilities	7535	Electricity	160	48.13%	10.63%	15.00%	26.25%	5.79	25.73
	7573	Gas Distribution	57	8.77%	22.81%	5.26%	63.16%	10.52	22.27
	7575	Multiutilities	22	27.27%	13.64%	13.64%	45.45%	7.27	18.87
			239	36.82%	13.81%	12.55%	36.82%	7.36	21.72
Banks	8355	Banks	231	31.60%	18.61%	12.99%	36.80%	4.40	12.47
			231	31.60%	18.61%	12.99%	36.80%	4.40	12.47
Insurance	8532	Full Line Insurance	25	28.00%	8.00%	36.00%	28.00%	5.56	12.51
	8536	Property & Casualty Insurance	72	26.39%	19.44%	16.67%	37.50%	8.19	20.10
	8538	Reinsurance	11	27.27%	9.09%	54.55%	9.09%	6.73	21.77
	8575	Life Insurance	43	27.91%	6.98%	34.88%	30.23%	7.30	14.58
			151	27.15%	13.25%	27.81%	31.79%	6.94	17.24
Financial Services	8733	Real Estate Holding & Development	63	25.40%	7.94%	33.33%	33.33%	4.16	17.19
	8737	Real Estate Investment Trusts	50	28.00%	18.00%	22.00%	32.00%	6.36	21.05
	8771	Asset Managers	19	31.58%	21.05%	21.05%	26.32%	14.00	11.78
	8773	Consumer Finance	28	7.14%	28.57%	17.86%	46.43%	7.06	12.89
	8775	Specialty Finance	27	11.11%	37.04%	18.52%	33.33%	7.50	9.49
	8777	Investment Services	28	21.43%	42.86%	21.43%	14.29%	6.12	10.78
			215	21.86%	22.33%	24.19%	31.63%	7.53	13.86
Technology	9533	Computer Services	46	4.35%	32.61%	41.30%	21.74%	9.91	8.46
	9537	Software	46	8.70%	43.48%	13.04%	34.78%	19.76	12.99
	9572	Computer Hardware	78	8.97%	23.08%	26.92%	41.03%	8.22	12.62
	9574	Electronic Office Equipment	21	14.29%	9.52%	33.33%	42.86%	7.00	4.69
	9576	Semiconductors	85	14.12%	25.88%	18.82%	41.18%	10.07	20.47
	9578	Telecommunications Equipment	50	12.00%	16.00%	34.00%	38.00%	2.34	7.24
			326	10.43%	26.07%	26.38%	37.12%	9.55	11.08

APPENDIX C

Performance Across Firm Sizes

Performance Record for the Period 2000–2004 Across Different Firm Sizes

Size	Number of Firms	Profitability Only	Growth Only	Profitable Growth	Neither	Weighted Average ROIC (%)	Weigted Average AGR (%)
X < 1B	1654	19.29%	17.71%	24.49%	38.51%	7.00	15.40
1B ≤ X < 5B	2218	20.87%	15.73%	28.00%	35.39%	8.20	15.19
5B ≤ X < 10B	469	21.32%	16.63%	26.87%	35.18%	8.18	14.99
10B ≤ X < 50B	458	25.98%	16.59%	20.52%	36.90%	8.04	13.42
50B ≤ X	85	23.53%	18.82%	29.41%	28.24%	8.06	14.94

APPENDIX D
Performance Across Regions

Performance Record for the Period 2000–2004 Across Major Geographies

Country	Number of Firms	Profitability Only	Growth Only	Profitable Growth	Neither	Weighted Average ROIC (%)	Weighted Average AGR (%)
UNITED STATES	1457	31.64%	12.83%	24.50%	31.02%	9.02	14.91
JAPAN	1136	7.31%	14.96%	6.95%	70.77%	2.95	7.75
UNITED KINGDOM	274	22.26%	17.52%	32.48%	27.74%	9.12	15.56
FRANCE	163	11.04%	26.38%	38.04%	24.54%	7.78	17.61
CANADA	150	20.00%	19.33%	36.00%	24.67%	8.44	19.69
GERMANY	136	19.12%	14.71%	33.82%	32.35%	8.90	16.60
ITALY	102	7.84%	41.18%	29.41%	21.57%	4.33	21.95

Major Firms in the Field Study

Performance Histories of the Major Firms in the Study

Company	Subsector	Sales USD Y2005	Emphasis	Year	AGR %	ROIC % 5 year average
		(Million)				
Royal Dutch Shell	Integrated Oil & Gas	306,731.00		Y2005	13.1487	17.8137
				(Data for one year only)		
Ericsson Telephone AB	Telecommunications Equipment	19,080.86	Profit	Y2005	-6.6228	3.4834
				Y2004	-2.8112	3.1134
Nestle	Food Products	69,153.25	Balanced	Y2005	7.0970	12.1658
				Y2004	10.5070	12.9649
Dow Chemicals Company	Commodity Chemicals	46,307.00	Balanced	Y2005	15.3427	8.5611
				Y2004	16.5918	7.1628
Medtronic Inc	Medical Equipment	10,054.60	Balanced	Y2005	14.9899	16.8310
				Y2004	17.1203	18.8800
Best Buy Company Inc	Specialty Retailers	27,433.00	Balanced	Y2005	17.2733	17.9658
				Y2004	19.7168	19.8456
Nokia Corporation	Telecommunications Equipment	40,414.79	Balanced	Y2005	7.3963	22.5187
				Y2004	15.7988	24.9983
Canon Inc	Electronic Office Equipment	31,798.00	Balanced	Y2005	6.1510	12.5737
				Y2004	6.3791	11.1785
Sharp Corp.	Consumer Electronics	23,696.88	Growth	Y2005	7.1345	3.4152
				Y2004	10.0201	2.8052

References

Chapter 1, "The Performance Dilemmas"

[1] C. Zook and P. Rogers, "In Pursuit of Growth," *European Business Journal*, 2001, 83–85.

[2] A. J. Slywotzky and R. Wise, "The Growth Crisis—and How to Escape It," *Harvard Business Review*, July 2002, 5–15.

[3] R. R. Wiggins and T. W. Ruefli, "Sustained Competitive Advantage: Temporal Dynamics and the Incidence and Persistence of Superior Economic Performance," *Organization Science*, 2002, 13(1): 82–105.

[4] B. S. Chakravarthy and N. Govinder, "Medtronic: Keeping Pace," Case 3-130, IMD, 2002.

[5] A. Slywotzky and R. Wise, *How to Grow When Markets Don't*, Warner Business Books, 2003.

[6] C. Zook, *Beyond the Core: Expand Your Market without Abandoning Your Roots*, Harvard Business School Publishing, 2004.

[7] G. Hamel and C. K. Prahalad, *Competing for the Future*, Harvard Business School Press, 1994.

[8] C. M. Christensen and M. E. Raynor, *The Innovator's Solution*, Harvard Business School, 2003.

[9] R. Foster and S. Kaplan, *Creative Destruction*, Currency, 2001.

Chapter 2, "Renewal Strategies"

[1] See G. Hamel, and C. K. Prahalad, *Competing for the Future* (Harvard Business School Publishing, 1994) for an early framework. Also see B. S. Chakravarthy, "Flexible Commitments," *Strategy and Leadership*, 24, 1996; R. Ramirez and J. Wallin, *Prime Movers* (John Wiley, 2000); or J. Canals, "How to Think about Corporate Growth," *European Management Journal*, 19(6), 2001.

[2] This stream of research, popularly called the resource-based view, has more recently been focusing on the dynamic capabilities of the firm and not just its static resources. Illustrative of the work being done in this area are the writings of J. Barney, "Strategic Factor Markets: Expectations, Luck, and Business Strategy," *Management Science*, 32(10), 1986. Also see M. A. Peteraf, "The Cornerstones of Competitive Advantage: A Resource-Based View," *Strategic Management Journal*, 14(3), 1993; D. J. Collis and C. A. Montgomery, "Competing on Resources," *Harvard Business Review*, 73(4), 1995; D. Teece, G. Pisano, and A. Shuen, "Dynamic Capabilities and Strategic Management," *Strategic Management Journal*, 18(7), 1997.

[3] M. E. Porter, *Competitive Advantage*, Free Press, 1986.

[4] Chris Zook, *Beyond the Core: Expand Your Market without Abandoning Your Roots,* Harvard Business School Publishing, 2004.

[5] It is pertinent to observe that Hamel and Prahalad urge firms to imagine their future and create it, assuring managers that there is not one future, but hundreds—as many prizes as runners. Companies such as Bausch & Lomb were perhaps victims of their own exaggerated sense of creativity. The imagined future must eventually face the hard reality of a market test. Here the prizes are limited. There are winners and losers.

[6] P. Lorange, "Managing Internal Growth at Nestlé: The Story of LC1," Case GM 840, IMD, 2003.

[7] See "3M Optical Systems: Managing Corporate Entrepreneurship," Case 9-395-017, Harvard Business School. Revised May 28, 1999.

Chapter 3, "Continuous Renewal"

[1] The quote and information about Samsung's strategy are from P. Lewis, "The Perpetual Crisis Machine," *Fortune,* September 5, 2005.

[2] B. S. Chakravarthy and H. Bourgeois, "Best Buy: Staying at the Top," Case 3-1430, IMD, 2004.

Chapter 4, "A Blended Approach"

[1] R. Bruner, "M&A under Scrutiny," *Electronic News,* December 13, 1999.

[2] The Boston Consulting Group, The Successful Value Creation Record of Acquisitive Growth Strategies, May 2004.

[3] The Boston Consulting Group, The Role of Alliances in Corporate Strategy, November 2005.

[4] Anonymous, "R&D Beats M&A," *Works Management,* 55(10), October 2002.

[5] G. K. Morbey and R. M. Reithner, "How R&D Affects Sales Growth, Productivity and Profitability," *Research Technology Management,* 33(3), May—June 1990.

[6] J-P Deschamps and A. Pahwa, "New Business Creation at Tetra Pak: Reinventing the Food Can," Case Study 3-1488, IMD, 2004.

[7] S. Meehan and J. Shaner, "Hilti France: Strategy Implementation," IMD Cases 3-0859/0860, 2000.

[8] See J. H. Dyer, P. Kale, and H. Singh, "When to Ally and When to Acquire," *Harvard Business Review,* July—August 2004.

[9] H. Chesbrough and D. Teece, "Organizing for Innovation: When Is Virtual Virtuous?" *Harvard Business Review,* 1, August 2002.

[10] Larry Huston and Nabil Sakkab, "Connect and Develop: Inside Procter & Gamble's New Model for Innovation," *Harvard Business Review,* 84(3), March 2006.

[11] P. C. Haspeslagh and D. B. Jemison, in *Managing Acquisitions* (Free Press, 1991), were among the first to propose a contingent approach.

[12] Y. Doz and G. Hamel outline this in their book, *The Alliance Advantage,* Harvard Business School Publishing, 1998.

[13] B. S. Chakravarthy and N. Govinder, "Medtronic: Keeping Pace," Case 3-130, IMD, 2002.

Chapter 5, "The Entrepreneur-Manager"

[1] P. Lorange, "Managing Internal Growth at Nestlé: The Story of LC1," Case GM 840, IMD, 2003.

[2] K. Kashani, "Innovation and Renovation: The Nespresso Story," Case M 543, IMD, 2003.

[3] This is a disguised name used throughout the book and not the real name of the entrepreneur-manager.

[4] P. Lorange, "Internal Entrepreneurship at Ericsson: Finding Opportunities and Mobilizing Talent," Case GM 783, IMD, 1999.

[5] B. S. Chakravarthy, "Internal Entrepreneurship at the Dow Chemical Company," Case 3-1117, IMD, 2003.

[6] B. S. Chakravarthy, "Nick Earle: The Plate Spinner," Case 3-1071, IMD, 2003.

Chapter 6, "Sponsoring Renewal"

[1] J. Walsh and J-P Deschamps, "Senseo: Establishing a New Standard in the Home Coffee Market," Case 5-0674, IMD, 2005.

[2] R. Simons, *Levers of Control,* Harvard Business School Publishing, 1994.

[3] S. Ghoshal, "Canon: Competing on Capabilities," Case 392-031-1, Insead. Our views here are also based on interviews with company executives.

Chapter 7, "Directing Renewal"

[1] James C. Collins and Jerry I. Porras, *Built to Last,* New York: HarperBusiness, 1994.

[2] Jim Collins, *Good to Great,* London: Random House Business Books, 2001.

[3] See B. S. Chakravarthy and N. Govinder, "Medtronic: Keeping Pace," IMD Case 3-1030, 2002.

[4] An interview that the authors had with D. Vasella in his offices in Basel, Switzerland, on February 5, 2004.
[5] R. J. Barnet and J. Cavanagh, *Global Dreams: Imperial Corporations and the New World Order,* Simon & Schuster, 1994.
[6] See K. Ichijo, "Be Sharp! Sharp's Innovation in the LCD Industry," Case 3-1554, IMD, 2005; and D. J. Collis, "Sharp Corporation: Technology Strategy," Harvard Business School, Case 9-793-064, 1995.
[7] P. Killing, "Nestlé's GLOBE Program (A): The Early Months," Case 3-1334, IMD, 2003; and "Nestlé's GLOBE Program (B): July Executive Board Meeting," Case 3-1335, IMD, 2003.
[8] D. Vasella, *Magic Cancer Bullet,* Harper Business, 2003. Gleevec is called Glivec outside of the United States and Canada.
[9] Warren Bennis, *On Becoming a Leader,* New York: Random House, 1998.

Chapter 8, "The Multiactor Process"
[1] Adapted from B. Chakravarthy, "The Process of Transformation: In Search of Nirvana," *European Management Journal,* 14(6), 529–539, 1996.

INDEX

O

P

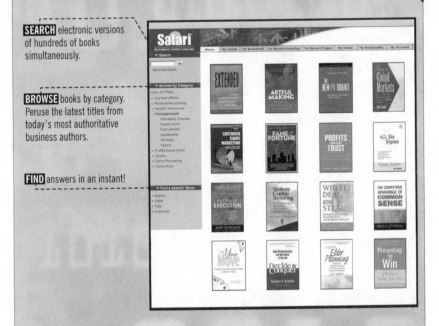

In five days, even Darwin would be shocked at how you've changed.

What's Your Story?
Storytelling to Move Markets, Audiences, People, and Brands
RYAN MATHEWS AND WATTS WACKER

Storytelling is a universal human activity. It is universal in that every society, at every stage of history, has told stories. It is human because stories are how people tell each other who they are; where they came from; how they are different from their neighbors; what they worship; and what they believe. Stories capture a people's memory of their past and their hopes for the future. Businesses tell stories all the time, but without the discipline of the trained storyteller. Storytelling has a wide variety of business applications, many of which go all but ignored today. In a commercial world where consumers are bombarded by a multitude of often conflicting stories, and where they are no longer satisfied with being members of a passive audience, it is more critical than ever that formal storytelling be adopted as a business tool. Not only do today's storytellers need to know how to craft a story, they now carry the added burden of crafting a context for that story, providing a back story that makes their main story credible. *What's Your Story?* offers business readers a comprehensive storytelling tool chest and practical help in executing a modern storytelling strategy in their companies.

ISBN 9780132277426, © 2008, 240 pp., $24.99 USA, $29.99 CAN

The Advantage-Makers
How Exceptional Leaders Win by Creating Opportunities Others Don't
STEVEN FEINBERG

Are you an Advantage-Maker? If not, odds are you will lose to someone who is. Advantage-Makers are those rare leaders who win more often because they know how to consistently transform challenging situations into the best possible outcomes. The best part is that becoming an Advantage-Maker will not require new resources or any of the other often expensive solutions that have been proposed over the years; it simply requires a shift in how leaders view and think about their company and their competitive environment.

The best leaders see things others don't: they spot overlooked opportunities, create undreamed of benefits, shift the odds in their favor, and influence breakthrough outcomes. *The Advantage-Makers* finally reveals how they do it, and how you can, too.

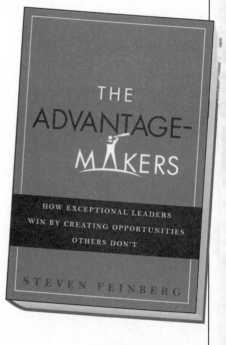

ISBN 9780132347785, © 2008, 304 pp., $27.99 USA, $34.99 CAN